Cambridge Elements

Elements in the Philosophy of Physics
edited by
James Owen Weatherall
University of California, Irvine

GLOBAL SPACETIME STRUCTURE

JB Manchak
University of California, Irvine

CAMBRIDGE
UNIVERSITY PRESS

CAMBRIDGE
UNIVERSITY PRESS

University Printing House, Cambridge CB2 8BS, United Kingdom

One Liberty Plaza, 20th Floor, New York, NY 10006, USA

477 Williamstown Road, Port Melbourne, VIC 3207, Australia

314–321, 3rd Floor, Plot 3, Splendor Forum, Jasola District Centre, New Delhi – 110025, India

79 Anson Road, #06–04/06, Singapore 079906

Cambridge University Press is part of the University of Cambridge.

It furthers the University's mission by disseminating knowledge in the pursuit of education, learning, and research at the highest international levels of excellence.

www.cambridge.org
Information on this title: www.cambridge.org/9781108819534
DOI: 10.1017/9781108876070

© JB Manchak 2020

First published 2020

A catalogue record for this publication is available from the British Library.

ISBN 978-1-108-81953-4 Paperback
ISSN 2632-413X (online)
ISSN 2632-4121 (print)

Global Spacetime Structure

Elements in the Philosophy of Physics

DOI: 10.1017/9781108876070
First published online: November 2020

JB Manchak
University of California, Irvine

Author for correspondence: JB Manchak, jmanchak@uci.edu

Abstract: This exploration of the global structure of spacetime within the context of general relativity examines the causal and singular structures of spacetime, revealing some of the curious possibilities that are compatible with the theory, such as "time travel" and "holes" of various types. Investigations into the epistemic and modal structures of spacetime highlight the difficulties in ruling out such possibilities, unlikely as they may seem at first. The upshot seems to be that what counts as a "physically reasonable" spacetime structure in modern physics is far from clear.

Keywords: spacetime, causality, singularities, underdetermination, extendibility

ISBNs: 9781108819534 (PB), 9781108876070 (OC)
ISSNs: 2632-413X (online), 2632-4121 (print)

Contents

1 Introduction

Global spacetime structure concerns the more foundational aspects of general relativity (e.g. the topological and causal structure of spacetime). Upon investigation, it is often the case that seemingly plausible statements concerning global spacetime structure turn out to be false. Indeed, even after the shift to a relativistic worldview it seems "we are still somewhat over-conditioned to Minkowski spacetime" (Geroch & Horowitz, 1979, p. 215). This Element can be viewed as a kind of manual to help us unlearn what we think we know concerning the global structure of spacetime. A large number of example spacetimes (with diagrams) are central to the presentation and serve to demonstrate just how much is permitted under general relativity. Along the way, open questions are highlighted and periodic exercises can be used to test one's understanding (sample solutions are given in the Appendix).

Section 2 concerns the basic structure of spacetime. A number of preliminary definitions are presented to get things started. The cut-and-paste method is also introduced, which is used throughout to construct a vast array of example spacetimes. Although such spacetimes may seem artificial in some sense, we find that "the mere existence of a space-time having certain global features suggests that there are many models – some perhaps quite reasonable physically – with very similar properties" (Geroch, 1971a, p. 78). Section 3 covers the causal structure of spacetime. It follows a fairly conventional presentation of the hierarchy of causality conditions (Hawking & Ellis, 1973; Wald, 1984). But some nonstandard topics of interest are also explored including the so-called Malament-Hogarth spacetimes allowing for "supertasks" of a certain kind (Earman & Norton, 1993).

Section 4 concerns the singular structure of spacetime. An example singularity theorem is presented showing a sense in which some "physically reasonable" spacetimes have singularities (cf. Hawking & Penrose, 1970). This raises a difficulty in how to sort singular spacetimes into physically reasonable and physically unreasonable varieties. Two families of conditions are investigated that are meant to do the sorting. One family primarily concerns the causal structure of spacetime and forbids "naked" singularities of various types; the other family primarily concerns the modal structure of spacetime and forbids spacetime "holes" of various types. After considering a rich collection of examples, the upshot seems to be that what counts as a physically reasonable spacetime is far from clear (Earman, 1995, p. 86).

As we leave old intuitions behind, a rather basic question arises: What can we know concerning the global structure of spacetime? Building on a trio of papers from Geroch (1977), Glymour (1977), and Malament (1977a),

Section 5 explores the epistemic structure of spacetime. It seems that even after we have (i) taken into consideration all possible observational data we could ever (even in principle) gather and (ii) inductively fixed the local features of any unobservable regions of spacetime, a type of "cosmic underdetermination" keeps us from pinning down the global structure of the universe. And if we take seriously the idea that we cannot come to know the global structure of spacetime through observation, queer possibilities present themselves. Does our universe allow for "time travel" of a certain kind? Do spacetime "holes" exist in our universe? This suggests that perhaps we have been too quick to discount as physically unreasonable some of the more peculiar global spacetime properties since, for all we know, such properties obtain in our own universe.

In Section 6, the modal structure of spacetime is explored through the lens of the inextendibility condition. This is the requirement that the universe be as large as possible relative to a standard background collection of spacetimes. But the inextendibility condition would seem to be physically significant only insofar as the background collection coincides with physically reasonable possibilities (Geroch, 1970a). And because what counts as a physically reasonable spacetime is not clear – especially given the underdetermination results just mentioned – it seems natural to consider various nonstandard definitions of inextendibility in a pluralistic way. Upon investigation, we find that foundational claims concerning inextendibility can fail to hold up under some modified definitions. For example, it can happen that a spacetime is "extendible" and yet has no "inextendible extension" – a strange state of affairs with the potential to clash with various Leibniz-inspired metaphysical principles in favor of the "maximality" of spacetime (Earman, 1995, p. 32). In addition, the demand for modified forms of inextendibility can lead to situations in which a spacetime is forced into having global properties of interest. A so-called time machine represents one example along these lines, but other "machine" spacetimes can also be studied (cf. Earman et al., 2016). Stepping back, we find that the prospect of a clear distinction between physically reasonable and physically unreasonable spacetimes is more elusive than ever.

2 Preliminaries

A (general relativistic) ***spacetime*** is a pair (M, g_{ab}) where M is a smooth, connected, Hausdorff, paracompact, n-dimensional ($n \geq 2$) manifold and g_{ab} is a smooth metric on M of Lorentz signature $(+, -, \ldots, -)$. Under the assumption of Einstein's equation (see p. 6), a spacetime is a model of general relativity and represents a possible universe compatible with the theory. Details concerning the relevant background mathematics (including the "abstract index" notation used throughout) can be found in Hawking and Ellis (1973), Wald (1984), or Malament (2012). Here, we follow Geroch & Horowitz (1979) in avoiding technical machinery whenever possible.

We begin with the notion of a ***manifold***, which, unless otherwise stated, is taken to be smooth, connected, Hausdorff, and paracompact (see the Appendix for basic topological definitions). All of the topological structure of a spacetime (M, g_{ab}) is given by the manifold M; it fully captures the shape of the model. Locally, a manifold looks like plain old $\mathbb{R}^n$ although globally it may have a very different structure. A number of manifolds are easy to visualize. For example, consider the sphere S^2. Despite its round shape, if one zooms in on the vicinity of any point, one finds it has the same topological structure as the plane $\mathbb{R}^2$ (see Figure 1). Other two-dimensional manifolds include the cylinder $S^1 \times \mathbb{R}$ and the torus $S^1 \times S^1$. In addition, the result of taking any manifold and removing from it a closed proper subset also counts as a manifold. For example, a new manifold $\mathbb{R}^2 - \{(0,0)\}$ can be constructed by excising the origin from the plane.

We say the n-dimensional manifolds M and N are ***diffeomorphic*** if there is a bijection $\varphi : M \to N$ such that both it and its inverse are smooth. Diffeomorphic manifolds have identical topological and smoothness properties. It turns out that every non-compact manifold of two dimensions or more admits some Lorentzian metric. One can also show that the compact manifold S^n for $n \geq 2$ admits a Lorentzian metric if and only if n is odd (Geroch & Horowitz, 1979). We also have the useful result that any manifold $M \times N$ admits a Lorentzian metric if either M or N does. And of course, if M admits a Lorentzian metric, then so does $M - C$ where C is any closed proper subset of M.

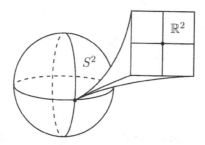

Figure 1 The sphere S^2 has the same topological structure as the plane $\mathbb{R}^2$ in the vicinity of each point.

Exercise 1   Find a manifold M and a point $p \in M$ such that M and $M - \{p\}$ are diffeomorphic.

Each point on a manifold represents an idealized possible event in spacetime (e.g. one's birth). The Lorentzian **metric** tells us how such events in spacetime are related to one another. Consider a spacetime (M, g_{ab}). At each point $p \in M$, the metric g_{ab} assigns to each vector ξ^a in the tangent space of p a length given by $\xi^a \xi^b g_{ab} = \xi^a \xi_a \in \mathbb{R}$. This creates a type of double cone structure in the tangent space of each point. Positive-length vectors are **timelike** and fall inside the cone, negative-length vectors are **spacelike** and fall outside the cone, and zero-length vectors are **null** and make up the boundary of the cone (see Figure 2).

One can think of the cone structure at each point as representing the speed of light in all directions there; timelike and spacelike vectors represent, respectively, velocities that are slower and faster than light. For this reason, we often refer to these structures as light cones in what follows. Now consider a smooth curve $\gamma : I \to M$ where I is some connected interval of $\mathbb{R}$. (In what follows, curves are understood to be smooth unless otherwise stated.) If each of its tangent vectors ξ^a is timelike according to g_{ab}, then we say the curve γ is **timelike**. Timelike curves represent the possible trajectories of massive objects. Analogous definitions can be given for **spacelike** and **null** curves; a **causal** curve has no spacelike tangent vectors (see Figure 3).

Associated with g_{ab} is a unique **derivative operator** ∇_a on M that is compatible with the metric in the sense that $\nabla_a g_{bc} = \mathbf{0}$. We say that a given curve $\gamma : I \to M$ is a **geodesic** if, for each each point along the curve, the tangent vector ξ^a is such that $\xi^a \nabla_a \xi^b = \mathbf{0}$. One can think of a geodesic as a curve that is as straight as possible according to a given metric. Timelike geodesics

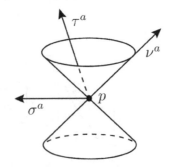

Figure 2 A three-dimensional double cone structure at the point p. A timelike vector τ^a, a null vector ν^a, and a spacelike vector σ^a are depicted.

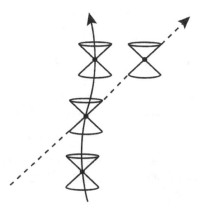

Figure 3 A pair of causal curves in a three-dimensional spacetime. One is timelike (solid line) and one is null (dotted line).

represent the possible trajectories of non-accelerating (freely falling) massive objects; null geodesics represent the possible trajectories of light. In any spacetime (M, g_{ab}), one can always find some open neighborhood $O \subseteq M$ around any point $p \in M$ such that any two points $q, r \in O$ can be connected by a unique geodesic whose image is contained in O.

Exercise 2 Find a spacetime (M, g_{ab}) and a pair of points $p, q \in M$ that can be connected by spacelike and null geodesics but not by a timelike geodesic.

A curve $\gamma : I \to M$ in a spacetime (M, g_{ab}) is **maximal** if there is no curve $\gamma' : I' \to M$ such that I is properly contained in I' and $\gamma(s) = \gamma'(s)$ for all $s \in I$. If a maximal geodesic $\gamma : I \to M$ is such that $I \neq \mathbb{R}$, then we say it is **incomplete**. A spacetime that harbors an incomplete geodesic is **geodesically incomplete**; otherwise it is **geodesically complete**. An incomplete timelike geodesic can be considered a type of singularity since it represents a possible trajectory of a freely falling massive object whose existence is cut short in either the past or future direction (cf. Geroch, 1968a; Curiel, 1999). By excising points from the manifold, one can easily create examples of geodesically incomplete spacetimes (see Figure 4).

Given a spacetime (M, g_{ab}), one can use its associated derivative operator ∇_a to define the **Riemann tensor** $R^a{}_{bcd}$ where $R^a{}_{bcd}\xi^b = -2\nabla_{[c}\nabla_{d]}\xi^a$ for all smooth vector fields ξ^a. Here, the square brackets indicate the antisymmetrization operation. In this case, we find that $-2\nabla_{[c}\nabla_{d]}\xi^a = -(\nabla_c\nabla_d - \nabla_d\nabla_c)\xi^a$ (see Malament, 2012, p. 33). The Riemann tensor encodes all of the curvature of spacetime at each point in M. A spacetime is **flat** if its Riemann tensor vanishes

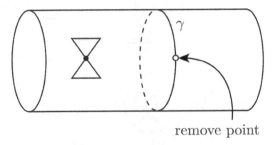

remove point

Figure 4 The timelike geodesic γ is maximal but incomplete since it cannot be extended through the missing point.

everywhere. The contraction of the Riemann tensor leads to the ***Ricci tensor*** $R_{ab} = R^c_{abc}$ and the ***Ricci scalar*** $R = R^a_a$ (see Malament, 2012, 84). The distribution of matter in spacetime can be represented by the ***energy-momentum tensor*** T_{ab} defined via Einstein's equation: $R_{ab} - (1/2)Rg_{ab} = 8\pi T_{ab}$. Here, we have ignored the possibility of a nonzero "cosmological constant" term in Einstein's equation (see Earman, 2001). Indeed, within the field of global structure there is a general lack of concern with the details of Einstein's equation; we find that "things which can happen in the absence of this equation can usually also happen in its presence" (Geroch & Horowitz, 1979, p. 215). If a spacetime is such that its corresponding energy-momentum tensor vanishes everywhere, then it is ***vacuum***. It turns out that any two-dimensional spacetime is vacuum (see Fletcher et al., 2018). In dimension three or greater, a spacetime is vacuum if and only if its associated Ricci tensor vanishes everywhere. Of course, any flat spacetime is necessarily vacuum.

We are now in a position to define ***Minkowski spacetime*** – it is any flat, geodesically complete spacetime with manifold $\mathbb{R}^n$. In standard (t,x) coordinates, two-dimensional Minkowski spacetime comes out as $(\mathbb{R}^2, g_{ab})$ where $g_{ab} = \nabla_a t \nabla_b t - \nabla_a x \nabla_b x$. This is the spacetime of special relativity and the vanilla model of general relativity. In what follows, we use Minkowski spacetime as our basic tool to construct various examples; we cut it, glue it, bend it, and warp it in order to get what we need. In a representation of Minkowski spacetime in standard coordinates, the light cones are uniformly oriented throughout and all geodesics appear as straight lines (see Figure 5).

Exercise 3   Find a flat spacetime such that every maximal timelike geodesic is incomplete but some maximal null and spacelike geodesics are complete.

Some spacetimes (M, g_{ab}) admit a continuous timelike vector field ξ^a on M and some do not. Those that do (e.g. Minkowski spacetime) allow for a

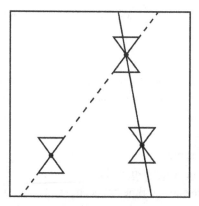

Figure 5 A timelike geodesic (solid line) and a null geodesic (dotted line) in two-dimensional Minkowski spacetime.

consistent global distinction between the "past" and "future" temporal directions since the continuous timelike vector field picks out one of two "lobes" of the light cone at each point. Such spacetimes are said to be ***time-orientable***. One can show that any spacetime (M, g_{ab}) is time-orientable if M is simply connected. A classic example of a spacetime that fails to be time-orientable can be constructed by starting with a Möbius strip manifold and orienting the light cones in such a way that any would-be continuous timelike vector field is flipped when transported around the strip (see Figure 6). In the following, we assume that spacetimes are time-orientable and that a temporal direction has been chosen. A causal curve $\gamma : I \to M$ in a spacetime (M, g_{ab}) is ***future-directed*** if its tangent vector at each point falls in or on the future lobe of the light cone or vanishes; an analogous definition can be given for ***past-directed*** causal curves. Unless otherwise stated, causal curves are understood to be future-directed.

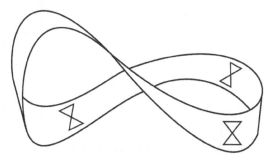

Figure 6 A spacetime that fails to be time-orientable since the flip in the Möbius strip precludes any continuous timelike vector field.

Exercise 4   Find a spacetime (M, g_{ab}) for some $M \subset \mathbb{R}^2$ that fails to be time-orientable.

Consider a spacetime (M, g_{ab}) and a pair of points p and q in M that, respectively, represent the past event of one's birth and the future event of one's reading of this sentence. One's trajectory through spacetime from the first event to the second can be represented by a future-directed timelike curve $\gamma : I \to M$ connecting p to q. The metric g_{ab} assigns a ***length*** $\|\gamma\| = \int (g_{ab} \xi^a \xi^b)^{1/2} ds$ to this curve by adding up the lengths of all the tangent vectors ξ^a along the curve. This length represents the elapsed time between p and q along γ. It follows that the elapsed time between any two events will depend on how one moves through spacetime from one to the other. Some trajectories with velocity vectors "close to the speed of light" will have a short elapsed time relative to others. Indeed, continuity considerations require that if two points can be connected by a timelike curve, then for any $\epsilon > 0$, there is a timelike curve connecting the points with length less than ϵ. It turns out that some spacetimes (e.g. Minkowski spacetime) are such that if two points can be connected by a timelike curve, then there is a longest curve connecting the points that must be a geodesic (see Figure 7).

A point $p \in M$ in a spacetime (M, g_{ab}) is a ***future endpoint*** of a future-directed causal curve $\gamma : I \to M$ if, for every open neighborhood O of p, there exists a point $s' \in I$ such that $\gamma(s) \in O$ for all $s > s'$. A ***past endpoint*** is defined analogously. We say that a causal curve is ***future-inextendible*** if it has no future endpoint and analogously for ***past-inextendible***. A causal curve is ***inextendible*** if it is both future-inextendible and past-inextendible. A causal curve that is inextendible must be maximal, but the converse is false. In Minkowski

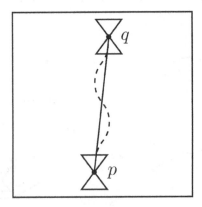

Figure 7 The points p and q can be connected by a short timelike curve (dotted line), but the longest such curve will be a geodesic (solid line).

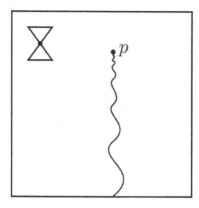

Figure 8 A maximal timelike curve with future endpoint p.

spacetime, a timelike curve can "wiggle" faster and faster as a future endpoint (which is not part of the curve) is approached (cf. Penrose, 1972, p. 3). The curve counts as maximal since any extension through the endpoint must fail to be smooth (see Figure 8).

Given an n-dimensional spacetime (M, g_{ab}), a set $S \subset M$ is a ***spacelike surface*** if S is an $(n - 1)$-dimensional sub-manifold of M such that every curve whose image is contained in S is spacelike. A set $S \subset M$ in a spacetime (M, g_{ab}) is ***achronal*** if no two points in S can be connected by a timelike curve. The ***edge*** of a closed, achronal set $S \subset M$ is the collection of points $p \in S$ for which every open neighborhood O of p contains points q and r such that future-directed timelike curves exist from q to p, from p to r, and from q to r where the last curve fails to intersect S (see Figure 9). A ***slice*** is a closed, achronal set with an empty edge. In Minkowski spacetime in standard (t, x) coordinates, each $t = $ constant surface counts as a slice. But not all spacetimes admit slices. For example, consider the spacetime $(S^1 \times \mathbb{R}, g_{ab})$ where $g_{ab} = \nabla_a t \nabla_b t - \nabla_a x \nabla_b x$ and $0 \leq t \leq 2\pi$; this is just Minkowski spacetime that has been "rolled up" along the time direction. Let this spacetime be called ***time-rolled Minkowski spacetime***. In an analogous way, one can also construct other two-dimensional models: ***space-rolled, null-rolled***, and ***(time and space)–rolled Minkowski spacetimes***.

Exercise 5 Find a spacelike surface in Minkowski spacetime that fails to be achronal.

A diffeomorphism $\varphi : M \to M'$ between the spacetimes (M, g_{ab}) and (M', g'_{ab}) is an ***isometry*** if $\varphi^*(g'_{ab}) = g_{ab}$ where φ^* is the map associated with φ, which,

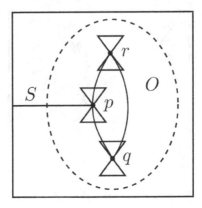

Figure 9 The point p is in the edge of the closed, achronal set S since every open neighborhood O of p contains points q and r such that future-directed timelike curves exist from q to p, from p to r, and from q to r where the last curve fails to intersect S.

for any point $p \in M$, pulls back the tensor g'_{ab} at $\varphi(p) \in M'$ to the tensor $\varphi^*(g'_{ab})$ at $p \in M$ (Malament, 2012, p. 36). Spacetimes (M, g_{ab}) and (M', g'_{ab}) are *isometric* if there is an isometry between them. Isometric spacetimes have fully equivalent structure and share all of the same physical properties; indeed, when no confusion arises, we often take isometric spacetimes to be the same spacetime in what follows. Consider the spacetimes (M, g_{ab}) and (M', g'_{ab}). If there is a proper subset O of M' such that (M, g_{ab}) and (O, g'_{ab}) are isometric, then we say that (M, g_{ab}) is *extendible* and (M', g'_{ab}) is an *extension* of (M, g_{ab}). A spacetime that is not extendible is *inextendible*.

Exercise 6 Find a pair of non-isometric spacetimes such that each counts as an extension of the other.

It turns out that every geodesically complete spacetime (e.g. Minkowski spacetime) is inextendible. But the other direction does not hold. To see this, consider Minkowski spacetime in standard (t, x) coordinates and remove two slits $S_n = \{(0, n) : n \leq x \leq n + 1/2\}$ for $n = 1, 2$. Excluding the four slit boundary points, identify the top edge of each slit with the bottom edge of the other (Hawking & Ellis, 1973, p. 58; Geroch, 1977, p. 89). The resulting spacetime is such that an observer entering one slit from below must emerge from the other slit from above. Because the four slit boundary points are "missing" from the spacetime, there are incomplete geodesics (see Figure 10). But one can show that this spacetime cannot be extended.

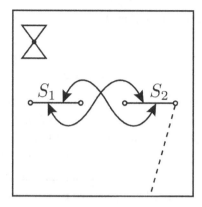

Figure 10 The top edge of the slit S_1 is identified with the bottom edge of the slit S_2 and vice versa. A maximal geodesic (dotted line) that approaches one of the four missing points must be incomplete.

Exercise 7   Find a flat, inextendible spacetime $(\mathbb{R}^2, g_{ab})$ that is not isometric to Minkowski spacetime.

Any spacetime with compact manifold must be inextendible (O'Neill, 1983, p. 155). Moreover, one can show (using Zorn's lemma) that every spacetime is either inextendible or has an inextendible extension (Geroch, 1970a, p. 277). In general, an extension to a given extendible spacetime is not unique. But given any inextendible spacetime (M, g_{ab}) and any point $p \in M$, every extension of the extendible spacetime $(M - \{p\}, g_{ab})$ is isometric to (M, g_{ab}) (see Manchak, forthcoming). So we do have unique extensions (up to isometry) in some cases.

    Spacetimes (M, g_{ab}) and (M', g'_{ab}) are ***locally isometric*** if for each point $p \in M$ there is an open set $O \subset M$ containing p and an open set $O' \subset M'$ such that (O, g_{ab}) and (O', g'_{ab}) are isometric, and, correspondingly, with the roles of (M, g_{ab}) and (M', g'_{ab}) interchanged. We say that a spacetime property is ***local*** if, given any pair of locally isometric spacetimes, one spacetime has the property if and only if the other does as well; a spacetime property is ***global*** if it is not local (Manchak, 2009). One can verify that the property of being vacuum comes out as local. On the other hand, consider two copies of Minkowski spacetime and remove a point from one of them. These spacetimes are locally isometric. But although Minkowski spacetime is geodesically complete by definition (and therefore inextendible), Minkowski spacetime with one point removed is clearly extendible (and therefore geodesically incomplete). So geodesic completeness and inextendibility count as global spacetime properties.

Exercise 8   Is being time-orientable a global property? Is being two-dimensional?

3 Causality

We begin an exploration of the causal structure of spacetime by defining a pair of two-place relations on M for every spacetime (M, g_{ab}). For each $p, q \in M$, we write $p \ll q$ if there is a future-directed timelike curve from p to q; we write $p < q$ if a future-directed causal curve exists from p to q. Immediately, we see that if $p \ll q$, then $p < q$. The other direction does not hold in general since, for example, a future-directed null geodesic from the point p to the point q in Minkowski spacetime will be such that $p < q$ but $p \not\ll q$ (see Figure 11). One can show that for any spacetime (M, g_{ab}) and any points $p, q \in M$, if $p < q$ and $p \not\ll q$, then any causal curve connecting p and q must be a null geodesic.

The relation $<$ is always reflexive: for any spacetime (M, g_{ab}) and any point $p \in M$, we have $p < p$. To see this, consider that one can always define a trivial curve $\gamma : I \rightarrow M$ to be such that $\gamma(s) = p$ for all $s \in I$; the curve has a vanishing tangent vector everywhere and therefore counts as a null curve that is both past and future directed. The relation $\ll$ can sometimes be reflexive as in time-rolled Minkowski spacetime (see Figure 12) and can sometimes fail to be reflexive as in Minkowski spacetime where $p \ll p$ for no point p. The relations $<$ and $\ll$ are always transitive (O'Neill, 1983, p. 402): for any spacetime (M, g_{ab}) and for any points $p, q, r \in M$, if both $p < q$ and $q < r$, it follows that $p < r$ (and analogously for the $\ll$ relation). Some spacetimes such as time-rolled Minkowski spacetime have symmetric relations $<$ and $\ll$: for any points $p, q \in M$, if $p < q$, then $q < p$ (and analogously for the $\ll$ relation). But in other

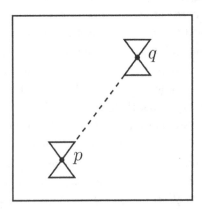

Figure 11 The points p and q can be connected by a future-directed causal curve (dotted line) but cannot be connected by a timelike curve.

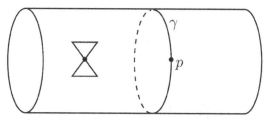

Figure 12 Time-rolled Minkowski spacetime is such that a future-directed timelike curve γ exists from any point p back to itself.

spacetimes – Minkowski spacetime is one example – one can find a pair of points $p, q \in M$, such that $p < q$ but $q \not< p$ (and analogously for the $\ll$ relation).

Exercise 9 Find a spacetime (M, g_{ab}) and points $p, q \in M$ such that $p \ll p$, $q \ll q$, and $p \ll q$ but $q \not\ll p$.

We say that a pair of spacetimes (M, g_{ab}) and (M, g'_{ab}) are **conformally equivalent** if there is some smooth, everywhere positive, scalar field $\Omega : M \to \mathbb{R}$ such that $g'_{ab} = \Omega^2 g_{ab}$. Here, the scalar field is called the **conformal factor**. Conformally equivalent spacetimes (M, g_{ab}) and (M, g'_{ab}) have identical causal structure in the sense that for all $p, q \in M$, $p < q$ in (M, g_{ab}) if and only if $p < q$ in (M, g'_{ab}) and analogously for the $\ll$ relation. One can show that if a pair of conformally equivalent spacetimes (M, g_{ab}) and (M, g'_{ab}) assign the same length $\|\gamma\|$ to every timelike curve $\gamma : I \to M$, then the two spacetimes are, in fact, isometric (Malament, 2012, p. 137).

When constructing spacetimes with particular properties, it is often useful to consider conformally equivalent versions of a simple model. Here is one famous example (Geroch, 1968a, p. 531). Suppose one wanted to find a spacetime with some timelike incomplete geodesics but no spacelike or null incomplete geodesics. Start with Minkowski spacetime (M, g_{ab}) in standard (t, x) coordinates and consider the conformally equivalent spacetime $(M, \Omega^2 g_{ab})$ where $\Omega : M \to \mathbb{R}$ is such that (i) $\Omega(t, x) = \Omega(t, -x)$, (ii) $\Omega = 1$ for $|x| > 1$, and (iii) $\Omega(t, 0) \to 0$ as $t \to \infty$. The symmetry of (i) ensures that the maximal timelike curve at $x = 0$ is a geodesic. From (iii), we know that this geodesic will be incomplete if Ω is chosen to approach zero sufficiently fast. But (ii) requires that any null or spacelike maximal geodesic must escape the region $|x| \leq 1$ in both directions and thus end up being complete (see Figure 13).

Consider a spacetime (M, g_{ab}) and a point $p \in M$. The **timelike future** of p is the set $I^+(p) = \{q : p \ll q\}$. Similarly, the **causal future** of p is the set $J^+(p) = \{q : p < q\}$; the **timelike past** $I^-(p)$ and **causal past** $J^-(p)$ are

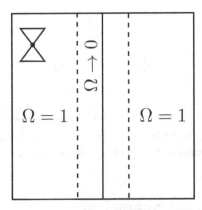

Figure 13 A maximal timelike geodesic (solid line) is incomplete due to the chosen conformal factor Ω, but any maximal null or spacelike geodesic is complete since it must escape the region between the dotted lines.

defined analogously. For any set $S \subseteq M$, we define $I^+(S)$ to be $\bigcup\{I^+(p) : p \in S\}$ and analogously for $I^-(S)$, $J^+(S)$, and $J^-(S)$. The causal (respectively, time-like) future of a point represents the region of spacetime that can be possibly influenced by particles (respectively, massive particles) at the point. For any $p \in M$, one can show that the regions $I^+(p)$ and $I^-(p)$ are open. But although the regions $J^+(p)$ and $J^-(p)$ can sometimes be closed (e.g. in Minkowski space-time), they are not closed in general. To see this, consider Minkowski spacetime in standard (t,x) coordinates and remove the point $(0,0)$. The point $p = (1,1)$ in the resulting spacetime is such that $J^-(p)$ is not closed (see Figure 14). A useful result states that for any $p,q,r \in M$, if either (i) $q \in J^+(p)$ and $r \in I^+(q)$ or (ii) $q \in I^+(p)$ and $r \in J^+(q)$, then $r \in I^+(p)$. And from this one can show that for any $p \in M$, the regions $I^+(p)$ and $J^+(p)$ share identical boundaries and closures. Analogous results hold for the past direction.

Exercise 10 Find a geodesically complete spacetime (M, g_{ab}) and a point $p \in M$ such that $J^-(p)$ is not closed.

We say a causal curve $\gamma : I \to M$ is *closed* if there are distinct points $s, s' \in I$ such that $\gamma(s) = \gamma(s')$ and γ has no vanishing tangent vectors. It is immediate that a spacetime (M, g_{ab}) has a closed timelike curve through a point $p \in M$ if and only if $p \in I^-(p)$. A closed timelike curve allows for "time travel" of a certain kind; a massive object may both begin and end a journey through spacetime at the very same event. A spacetime free of closed timelike curves satisfies *chronology*. The *chronology-violating region* of a spacetime (M, g_{ab}) is the (necessarily open) set $\{p \in M : p \in I^-(p)\}$. It has been conjectured that

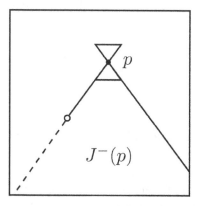

Figure 14 The point p is such that $J^-(p)$ is not closed. No future-directed causal curve exists from any point on the dotted line to p due to the missing point.

all physically reasonable spacetimes must have an empty chronology-violating region (cf. Hawking, 1992).

Minkowski spacetime satisfies chronology, but time-rolled Minkowski spacetime does not. Let (M, g_{ab}) be time-rolled Minkowski spacetime in (t, x) coordinates. The curve $\gamma: [0, 2\pi] \to M$ defined by $\gamma(s) = (s, 0)$ is a closed time-like geodesic. But not all spacetimes with closed timelike curves have closed timelike geodesics (Gödel, 1949). It turns out that if a spacetime (M, g_{ab}) is such that M is a compact manifold, then it must have a non-empty chronology-violating region (Geroch, 1967). The converse does not hold, however; indeed, one can find a chronology-violating spacetime with the manifold $\mathbb{R}^n$ for all $n \geq 3$. But given any non-compact manifold of two dimensions or more, one can find a chronological spacetime with that underlying manifold (Penrose, 1968). A spacetime (M, g_{ab}) is **totally vicious** if its chronology-violating region is all of M. It is easy to verify that time-rolled Minkowski spacetime is totally vicious. One can show that if (M, g_{ab}) is totally vicious, then for all $p \in M$ we have $I^-(p) = I^+(p) = M$ (Minguzzi, 2019, p. 113).

A spacetime satisfies **causality** if it is free of closed causal curves. It is immediate that any causal spacetime is chronological. But one can easily construct spacetimes that satisfy chronology but not causality; for example, consider null-rolled Minkowski spacetime (see Figure 15). One can show that a spacetime (M, g_{ab}) satisfies causality if and only if $J^+(p) \cap J^-(p) = \{p\}$ for all $p \in M$. A spacetime (M, g_{ab}) satisfies **distinguishability** if, for all distinct $p, q \in M$, both $I^+(p) \neq I^+(q)$ and $I^-(p) \neq I^-(q)$ hold. A spacetime satisfying distin-guishability must satisfy causality and moreover cannot have "almost" closed causal curves of a certain kind. In particular, we find that a spacetime (M, g_{ab})

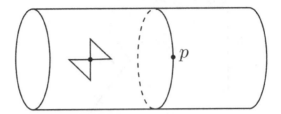

Figure 15 A closed null curve in a chronological spacetime.

satisfies distinguishability if and only if, for all $p \in M$ and all sufficiently small open sets O containing p, there is neither a future-directed nor a past-directed timelike curve that begins at p, leaves O, and returns to O (Malament, 2012, p. 133).

Consider spacetimes (M, g_{ab}) and (M', g'_{ab}) that satisfy distinguishability. If there is a bijection $\theta : M \to M'$ such that for all $p, q \in M$ we have $p \ll q$ if and only if $\theta(p) \ll \theta(q)$, then the spacetimes are conformally equivalent (Malament, 1977b). This means that, since the manifolds M and M' must be diffeomorphic, if the causal structure of spacetime is sufficiently nice, then that structure alone determines the shape of the universe completely.

Exercise 11   Find a causal spacetime (M, g_{ab}) and a discontinuous bijection $\theta : M \to M$ such that for all $p, q \in M$, $p \ll q$ if and only if $\theta(p) \ll \theta(q)$.

We say that a spacetime (M, g_{ab}) satisfies **strong causality** if, for all points $p \in M$ and all sufficiently small open sets $O \subseteq M$ containing p, there is no future-directed timelike curve that begins in O, leaves O, and returns to O (Malament, 2012, p. 134). Any spacetime that satisfies strong causality also satisfies distinguishability. To see that the converse does not hold, consider time-rolled Minkowski spacetime in (t, x) coordinates. One can delete the slits $S_1 = \{(0, x) : x \leq 1\}$ and $S_1 = \{(1, x) : 0 \leq x\}$ from the manifold so that distinguishability is saved but strong causality is not (see Figure 16). If a spacetime (M, g_{ab}) satisfies strong causality, then for every compact set $K \subset M$, a causal curve $\gamma : I \to K$ must have both past and future endpoints in K. So a strongly causal spacetime does not permit a (future or past) inextendible causal curve to be trapped within a compact region.

A spacetime (M, g_{ab}) satisfies **stable causality** if there is a continuous time-like vector field ξ^a on M such that the spacetime $(M, g_{ab} + \xi_a \xi_b)$ satisfies chronology. This means that a stably causal spacetime remains free of closed timelike curves even if all of the light cones are opened by a small amount at each point. One can show that any simply connected, two-dimensional

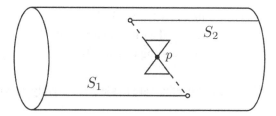

Figure 16 The removed slits S_1 and S_2 are chosen so that the spacetime is distinguishing but not strongly causal at the point p.

spacetime is stably causal (Minguzzi & Sánchez, 2008). Any spacetime that satisfies stable causality also satisfies strong causality, but not the other way around. Indeed, one can define an infinite number of nonequivalent causal levels between strong causality and stable causality (Carter, 1971). We say that a spacetime (M, g_{ab}) admits a ***global time function*** if there is a smooth scalar field $t : M \to \mathbb{R}$ such that, for any distinct points $p, q \in M$, if $p < q$, then $t(p) < t(q)$. One can think of the function t as assigning a time to every point in M such that it increases along every nontrivial future-directed causal curve. Remarkably, one can show that a spacetime satisfies stable causality if and only if it admits a global time function (Hawking, 1969).

Exercise 12   Find a spacetime that satisfies strong causality but violates stable causality.

We say a spacetime (M, g_{ab}) is ***reflecting*** if for all $p, q \in M$, p is in the closure of $J^-(q)$ if and only if q is in the closure of $J^+(p)$ (cf. Kronheimer & Penrose, 1967). One can show that a spacetime (M, g_{ab}) is reflecting if and only if the following holds: for all $p, q \in M$, $I^+(p) \subseteq I^+(q)$ if and only if $I^-(q) \subseteq I^-(p)$ (Hawking & Sachs, 1974). A useful result shows that a reflecting spacetime that is not totally vicious must be chronological (Clarke & Joshi, 1988). A spacetime satisfies ***causal continuity*** if it is both distinguishing and reflecting. In a causally continuous spacetime, points that are close must have similarly close timelike pasts and futures. Every causally continuous spacetime must be stably causal, but the other direction does not hold.

A spacetime (M, g_{ab}) is ***causally closed*** if for all $p \in M$, the sets $J^+(p)$ and $J^-(p)$ are closed. Every causally closed spacetime will be reflecting (Minguzzi, 2019, p. 110). On the other hand, Minkowski spacetime with a point removed is reflecting but not causally closed. We say a spacetime satisfies ***causal simplicity*** if it satisfies causality and is causally closed. One can show that any causally simple spacetime must be causally continuous, but not the other way around (Hawking & Sachs, 1974). In dimension three or more, if a spacetime is not totally vicious, then it is causally simple if and only if it is causally closed (Hounnonkpe & Minguzzi, 2019).

Exercise 13   Find a spacetime that satisfies stable causality but violates causal continuity.

A spacetime (M, g_{ab}) is **causally compact** if for all $p, q \in M$, the region $J^-(p) \cap J^+(q)$ is compact. Any causally compact spacetime must be causally closed and therefore reflecting. But the $x > 0$ portion of Minkowski spacetime in standard (t, x) coordinates shows that a causally closed spacetime need not be causally compact. The so-called transverse ladder of causal conditions can be summarized as follows: causal compactness $\Rightarrow$ causal closedness $\Rightarrow$ reflectivity (Minguzzi, 2019, p. 142). All three of these conditions can be satisfied in causally misbehaved models such as the totally vicious (time and space)-rolled Minkowski spacetime. But under the assumption of various minimal causal conditions, the satisfaction of any of the transverse ladder conditions ensures an extremely well-behaved causal structure. As we have seen, any reflecting and distinguishing spacetime is causally continuous (and thus stably causal) and any causally closed and causal spacetime is causally simple (and thus causally continuous). Let us now consider the case of causal compactness.

We say that a spacetime satisfies **global hyperbolicity** if it satisfies causality and is causally compact (Bernal & Sánchez, 2007). In dimension three or more, we find that if a spacetime is either (i) non-compact or (ii) not totally vicious, then it is globally hyperbolic if and only if it is causally compact (Hounnonkpe & Minguzzi, 2019). Any globally hyperbolic spacetime is causally simple, but there are spacetimes showing that the converse does not hold. Stepping back, the hierarchy of causal conditions considered here can be summarized as follows: global hyperbolicity $\Rightarrow$ causal simplicity $\Rightarrow$ causal continuity $\Rightarrow$ stable causality $\Rightarrow$ strong causality $\Rightarrow$ distinguishability $\Rightarrow$ causality $\Rightarrow$ chronology $\Rightarrow$ non-totally vicious.

One example of a spacetime that is causally simple but not globally hyperbolic is is **anti-de Sitter spacetime** – a model with manifold $\mathbb{R}^n$ and light cones that open up rapidly as they approach spatial infinity (see Figure 17). In (t, x) coordinates, two-dimensional anti-de Sitter spacetime comes out as $(\mathbb{R}^2, g_{ab})$ where $g_{ab} = \cosh^2 x \nabla_a t \nabla_b t - \nabla_a x \nabla_b x$.

The timelike past of every point in anti-de Sitter spacetime contains the image of a past-extendible timelike curve with infinite length. This is a curious property that seems to permit a "supertask" of a certain kind (Earman &

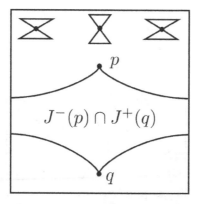

Figure 17 Anti-de Sitter spacetime is causally simple but not globally hyperbolic since the points p and q are such that the region $J^-(p) \cap J^+(q)$ is not compact.

Norton, 1993; Manchak & Roberts, 2016). Let us say that a spacetime (M, g_{ab}) is **Malament-Hogarth** if there is a point $p \in M$ and a past-extendible timelike curve $\gamma : I \to M$ such that $\|\gamma\| = \infty$ and the image of γ is contained in $I^-(p)$. In such a spacetime, an observer at the event p can "see" an observer along γ who has an infinite amount of future time in which to complete a "super task" such as checking all possible counterexamples to Goldbach's conjecture (i.e. the claim that every even integer greater than two is the sum of two primes). It is immediate that any spacetime that violates chronology will be Malament-Hogarth. And although one can find causally simple spacetimes that are Malament-Hogarth (e.g. anti-de Sitter spacetime), no globally hyperbolic ones exist (Hogarth, 1992).

Exercise 14   Find a Malament-Hogarth spacetime that is flat and satisfies chronology.

To get a better grip on the physical significance of global hyperbolicity, we turn to an equivalent formulation of the condition that concerns causal determinism of a certain kind. Consider a spacetime (M, g_{ab}) and set $S \subseteq M$. We define the **future domain of dependence** of S, denoted $D^+(S)$, to be the set of points $p \in M$ such that every past-inextendible causal curve through p intersects S. The **past domain of dependence** is defined analogously. The full **domain of dependence** of S is the set $D(S) = D^-(S) \cup D^+(S)$. Since any causal influence at a point in $D(S)$ must register on the set S, one can think of the physical situation on $D(S)$ as fully determined by the physical situation on S (Choquet-Bruhat & Geroch, 1969; Earman, 1986). In Minkowski spacetime,

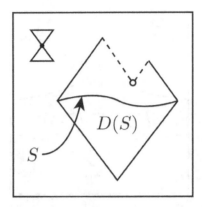

Figure 18 The domain of dependence $D(S)$ of a closed, achronal surface S in Minkowski spacetime with a point removed. Points on the dotted line are in the boundary of $D(S)$ but not in $D(S)$ itself.

the domain of dependence of a closed, achronal surface will often be diamond shaped; in Minkowski spacetime with a point removed, a notch can appear (see Figure 18).

Exercise 15 In Minkowski spacetime (M, g_{ab}), find slices $S, S' \subset M$ such that $D(S) \cap D(S') = \varnothing$ but $D(S) \cup D(S') = M$.

If a closed, achronal set $S \subset M$ in a spacetime (M, g_{ab}) is such that $D(S) = M$, then we say S is a ***Cauchy surface***. The physical situation on a Cauchy surface would seem to determine the physical situation everywhere in spacetime. Remarkably, one can show that a spacetime satisfies global hyperbolicity if and only if it admits a Cauchy surface; moreover, a globally hyperbolic spacetime (M, g_{ab}) will be such that M is homeomorphic to $\mathbb{R} \times N$ where $N \subset M$ is any Cauchy surface (Geroch, 1970b). This captures a sense in which global hyperbolicity forbids topology change of a certain kind (cf. Geroch, 1967). For Minkowski spacetime in standard (t, x) coordinates, each t = constant slice is a Cauchy surface. On the other hand, Minkowski spacetime with a point removed fails to have a Cauchy surface (see Figure 19).

Exercise 16 Find a manifold M that admits a Lorentzian metric but is such that every spacetime (M, g_{ab}) fails to have a Cauchy surface.

Given a spacetime (M, g_{ab}) and a closed, achronal set $S \subset M$, the ***future Cauchy horizon*** of S is the region $H^+(S)$ defined by taking the closure of $D^+(S)$ and

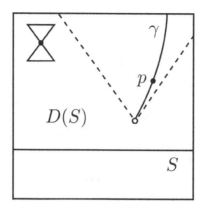

Figure 19 The slice S is not a Cauchy surface. The point p is not contained in $D(S)$ since the inextendible timelike curve γ passing through p approaches the missing point and thereby fails to intersect S.

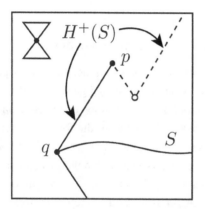

Figure 20 The future Cauchy horizon $H^+(S)$ of the closed, achronal surface S. The point p is the future endpoint of a null geodesic contained in $H^+(S)$ that has past endpoint q on the edge of S; the point p is also the future endpoint of a past-inextendible null geodesic contained in $H^+(S)$ that emerges from the missing point.

removing the points in $I^-(D^+(S))$. The **past Cauchy horizon** is defined analogously. One can show that $H^+(S)$ and $H^-(S)$ are both closed and achronal. In addition, every $p \in H^+(S)$ is the future endpoint of some null geodesic contained in $H^+(S)$ that is either past-inextendible or has a past endpoint on the edge of S (see Figure 20). Analogous results hold for $H^-(S)$. The full **Cauchy horizon** of S is the set $H(S) = H^+(S) \cup H^-(S)$. For any S that is closed and achronal, we find that $H(S)$ is the boundary of $D(S)$ and therefore closed. Moreover, for any non-empty S that is closed and achronal, $H(S)$ is empty if and only if S is a Cauchy surface.

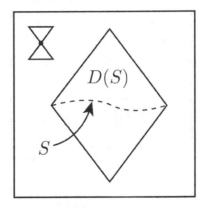

Figure 21 If the dominant energy condition is satisfied and $T_{ab} = \mathbf{0}$ on some achronal set S, then $T_{ab} = \mathbf{0}$ throughout $D(S)$.

4 Singularities

The various singularity theorems show senses in which a physically reasonable spacetime can have incomplete timelike geodesics (Penrose, 1965; Hawking & Penrose, 1970). To obtain such results, one must suppose some local constraint on the distribution of matter in the form of "energy conditions" (see Curiel, 2017). We say a spacetime (M, g_{ab}) satisfies the **weak energy condition** if, for all timelike vectors ξ^a at each point in M, we have $T_{ab}\xi^a\xi^b \geq 0$. This condition asserts that energy density cannot be negative. A spacetime satisfies the **strong energy condition** if, for all timelike vectors ξ^a at each point in M we have $(T_{ab} - \frac{1}{2}Tg_{ab})\xi^a\xi^b \geq 0$ for $T = T^a{}_a$. This condition asserts that "gravity attracts." Finally, a spacetime satisfies the **dominant energy condition** if it satisfies the weak energy condition and, in addition, for all timelike vectors ξ^a at each point in M, the vector $T^{ab}\xi_a$ is causal. This condition asserts that matter cannot travel faster than light. Indeed, one can show that if a spacetime (M, g_{ab}) satisfies the dominant energy condition and T_{ab} vanishes on some achronal set $S \subset M$, then T_{ab} vanishes on all of $D(S)$ (see Figure 21).

It is immediate that every vacuum spacetime (e.g. a flat or two-dimensional spacetime) satisfies all of the energy conditions. Let us now restrict attention to four-dimensional spacetimes (M, g_{ab}) satisfying the **constant curvature** condition: $R_{abcd} = (1/12)R(g_{ac}g_{bd} - g_{ad}g_{bc})$ (see Hawking & Ellis, 1973, p. 124). One can show that spacetimes satisfying the constant curvature condition must have a constant Ricci scalar R. Examples of such spacetimes include Minkowski spacetime for which $R = 0$, anti-de Sitter spacetime for which $R < 0$, and de Sitter spacetime for which $R > 0$ (see p. 35). A four-dimensional spacetime satisfying the constant curvature condition is such that $T_{ab} = -(1/32\pi)Rg_{ab}$, which provides an easy way to construct spacetimes violating one or more of the energy conditions. For example, a four-dimensional version of anti-de Sitter spacetime for which $R = -32\pi$ is such that $T_{ab} = g_{ab}$ and $T = T^a{}_a = n = 4$, showing that the strong energy condition must be violated.

Exercise 17   Find a spacetime that satisfies the strong energy condition but violates the weak energy condition.

We say a spacetime satisfies the **generic condition** if each causal geodesic with tangent ξ^a encounters some effective curvature in the sense that there is a point at which $\xi_{[a}R_{b]mn[c}\xi_{d]}\xi^m\xi^n \neq \mathbf{0}$. Only spacetimes with very special symmetries (e.g. any flat spacetime) will fail to be generic. If a spacetime satisfies the generic condition and is such that $R_{ab}\xi^a\xi^b \geq 0$ for all timelike vectors ξ^a – a requirement that is equivalent to the strong energy condition in four dimensions – we find a sense in which nearby timelike geodesics will tend to "cross" if they are complete (Geroch & Horowitz, 1979, p. 264). If a timelike geodesic is crossed in this way, one can always find a pair of points along it and a timelike curve connecting the points that has a longer length than the geodesic (see Figure 22).

We see that if a spacetime is four-dimensional and satisfies the generic and strong energy conditions, there will be a timelike geodesic that is either incomplete or does not maximize length in the sense just given. One can rule out the latter possibility by appealing to various global properties of interest. For example, here is a singularity theorem along these lines: any four-dimensional,

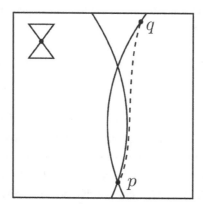

Figure 22 A timelike curve (dotted line) from p to q that cuts the corner near the crossing timelike geodesics (solid lines) has a longer length than the geodesic from p to q.

stably causal spacetime with compact slice that also satisfies the generic and strong energy conditions must have an incomplete timelike geodesic (Geroch & Horowitz, 1979, p. 265).

Exercise 18   Find a four-dimensional, stably causal spacetime with compact slice that satisfies the strong energy condition but is geodesically complete.

Because the singularity theorems show senses in which physically reasonable spacetimes can be geodesically incomplete, a difficulty arises in how to rule out pathological examples. Consider a spacetime (M, g_{ab}) and any point $p \in M$; how does one prohibit the seemingly artificial spacetime $(M - \{p\}, g_{ab})$? Requiring geodesic completeness will do the job, but this route is too heavy-handed given the singularity theorems. Instead, several other interrelated global conditions (e.g. inextendibility) have been suggested – none entirely satisfactory – to sort singular spacetimes into physically reasonable and physically unreasonable varieties. Let's take a look at a few examples.

We first consider a pair of definitions concerning so-called naked singularities that primarily concern the causal structure of spacetime. We say a future-inextendible causal geodesic $\gamma : I \to M$ is *future-incomplete* if there is a $r \in \mathbb{R}$ such that $r > s$ for all $s \in I$; a *past-incomplete* geodesic is defined analogously. A spacetime (M, g_{ab}) has a *detectable naked singularity* if there is a point $p \in M$ and a future-incomplete timelike geodesic $\gamma : I \to M$ such that the image of γ is contained in $\Gamma^-(p)$ (cf. Geroch & Horowitz, 1979, p. 274). In such a spacetime, the singularity is naked in the sense that an observer at p can see it. It is not difficult to verify that a spacetime with a point removed from its manifold will always have a detectable naked singularity (see Figure 23). One can also show that any spacetime with a detectable naked singularity will not be globally hyperbolic.

Exercise 19   Find a causally simple spacetime with detectable naked singularity.

A second type of naked singularity concerns the evolution of some initial data. We say a spacetime (M, g_{ab}) has an *evolved naked singularity* if there is a slice $S \subset M$ and a point $p \in H^+(S)$ such that the region $\Gamma^-(p) \cap S$ has compact closure. Here, the requirement that $\Gamma^-(p) \cap S$ have compact closure ensures that the slice S is not poorly chosen; for Minkowski spacetime in standard (t, x) coordinates, a poorly chosen slice includes the hyperboloid $S = \{(t, x) : t = -(x^2 + 1)^{1/2}\}$, which has a non-empty future Cauchy horizon (cf. Earman, 1995, p. 75). Minkowski spacetime with one point removed is an

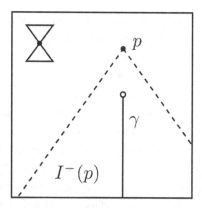

Figure 23 The point p is such that the future-incomplete timelike geodesic γ approaching the missing point is contained in the region $I^-(p)$.

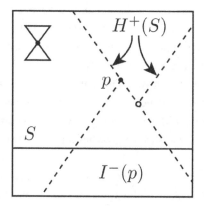

Figure 24 Due to the missing point, the slice S is such that there is a point $p \in H^+(S)$ for which $I^-(p) \cap S$ has compact closure.

example of a spacetime with an evolved naked singularity (see Figure 24). A spacetime with an evolved naked singularity need not have a detectable naked singularity and vice versa. But as before, any globally hyperbolic spacetime is free of evolved naked singularities.

Exercise 20 Find a spacetime with detectable naked singularity but no evolved naked singularity; find a spacetime with an evolved naked singularity but no detectable naked singularity.

A number of cosmic censorship conjectures have been suggested that serve to rule out nakedly singular spacetimes of various types including the two considered here. One quite strong version of this conjecture that precludes both detectable and evolved naked singularities is simply the assertion that all physically reasonable spacetimes must be globally hyperbolic (Penrose, 1969, 1979). But this position seems far from secure (Earman, 1995; Penrose, 1999).

Other conditions used to rule out physically unreasonable singularities concern the modal structure of spacetime; they rule out spacetime "holes" in the sense that they require that spacetime be as large as possible in various ways (cf. Earman, 1989, pp. 159–163). Inextendibility is one example of this type of condition. But inextendibility alone is not strong enough to rule out all examples of seemingly artificial singularities (recall Figure 10). To handle many of these other cases, another condition can be used. We say a spacetime (M, g_{ab}) is **hole-free** if, for every achronal surface $S \subset M$ and every isometric embedding $\varphi : D(S) \to M'$ into a spacetime (M', g'_{ab}), we have $\varphi[D(S)] = D(\varphi[S])$ (Geroch, 1977, p. 87). It is immediate that Minkowski spacetime with a point removed is not hole-free since the domain of dependence of some achronal surfaces could have been larger in Minkowski spacetime (see Figure 25).

Despite the intuitive appeal of the hole-freeness condition, a surprising result shows that Minkowski spacetime actually fails to satisfy it (Krasnikov, 2009). Take an achronal surface in two-dimensional Minkowski spacetime that has an open domain of dependence and isometrically embed it into space-rolled Minkowski spacetime. If the embedding is well chosen, the domain of dependence of the image of the surface now has a portion of its boundary included (see Figure 26).

One can fix up the definition of hole-freeness in a variety of ways (cf. Minguzzi, 2012). Consider a globally hyperbolic spacetime (M, g_{ab}) and an

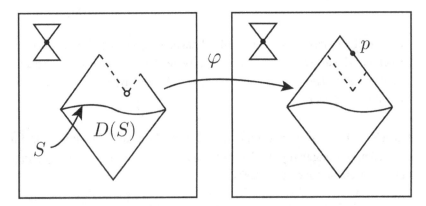

Figure 25 Due to the missing point, the achronal surface S is such that $D(S)$ can be isometrically embedded via φ in such a way that a point p is contained in $D(\varphi[S])$ but not in $\varphi[D(S)]$.

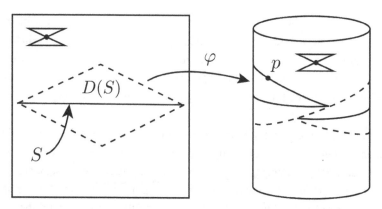

Figure 26 The achronal surface S is such that $D(S)$ can be isometrically embedded via φ in such a way that a point p is contained in $D(\varphi[S])$ but not in $\varphi[D(S)]$.

isometric embedding $\varphi : M \to M'$ into a spacetime (M', g'_{ab}). We say (M', g'_{ab}) is an ***effective extension*** of (M, g_{ab}) if, for some Cauchy surface S in (M, g_{ab}), $\varphi[M]$ is a proper subset of the interior of $D(\varphi[S])$ and $\varphi[S]$ is achronal. We say a spacetime (M, g_{ab}) is ***hole-free**** if, for every $K \subseteq M$ such that (K, g_{ab}) is a globally hyperbolic spacetime with Cauchy surface S, if (K', g_{ab}) is not an effective extension of (K, g_{ab}) where K' is the interior of $D(S)$, then (K, g_{ab}) has no effective extension. One intuitively satisfying consequence of this definition is this: for any spacetime (M, g_{ab}) and any point $p \in M$, the spacetime $(M - \{p\}, g_{ab})$ is not hole-free* (cf. Minguzzi, 2012). It is not difficult to see that a hole-free* spacetime need not be inextendible and vice versa. But one can show that a spacetime is hole-free* if it is either (i) inextendible and globally hyperbolic or (ii) geodesically complete (Manchak, 2014a). It is an open question whether global hyperbolicity in (i) can be weakened to causal simplicity (cf. Minguzzi, 2012). We do know that the geodesic completeness condition in (ii) can be weakened significantly to a type of local inextendibility condition (see p. 28)

Exercise 21   Find an inextendible, causally continuous spacetime that is not hole-free*.

Let us consider one more of the modal conditions used to rule out physically unreasonable singularities. We say a spacetime (M, g_{ab}) is ***locally inextendible*** if, for every open set $O \subset M$ with non-compact closure in M and every isometric embedding $\varphi : O \to M'$ into a spacetime (M', g'_{ab}), $\varphi[O]$ does not have compact closure in M' (Hawking & Ellis, 1973, p. 59). To see the definition at work, consider Minkowski spacetime (M, g_{ab}), an open set $O \subset M$ with compact closure in M, and point $p \in O$. The spacetime $(M - \{p\}, g_{ab})$ will fail to be locally inextendible since the open set $O - \{p\}$ has non-compact closure in $M - \{p\}$, but the inclusion map $\varphi : O - \{p\} \rightarrow M$ into Minkowski spacetime is an isometric embedding and $\varphi[O - \{p\}]$ has compact closure in M.

As with the condition hole-freeness, it turns out that local inextendibility is much stronger than had been supposed; indeed, not even Minkowski spacetime can satisfy it (Beem, 1980). In Minkowski spacetime in standard (t, x) coordinates, consider a curve starting at the point $(1, 0)$, which asymptotically approaches the line $t = 0$. Consider a small open set around the curve that becomes thinner as $t = 0$ is approached; this set has non-compact closure but can be isometrically embedded like a "spiral" into space-rolled Minkowski spacetime such that the closure of its image is compact (see Figure 27).

The condition of locally inextendibility can be fixed in a number of ways; here we consider just one (cf. Ellis & Schmidt, 1977, p. 928). We say a spacetime (M, g_{ab}) is ***locally inextendible*** * if, for every future-incomplete or past-incomplete timelike geodesic $\gamma : I \rightarrow M$, and every open set $O \subseteq M$ containing the image of γ, there is no isometric embedding $\varphi : O \rightarrow M'$ into some other spacetime (M', g'_{ab}) such that the curve $\varphi \circ \gamma : I \rightarrow M'$ has future and past endpoints. A locally inextendible* spacetime is sometimes called an effectively complete spacetime. We find that any geodesically complete spacetime will be locally inextendible* but the other direction does not hold. A useful result shows that any locally inextendible* spacetime must be both inextendible and hole-free* (Manchak, 2014a).

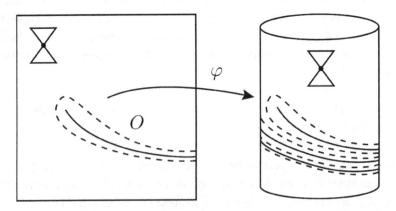

Figure 27 The open set O has non-compact closure but can be isometrically embedded via φ in such a way that $\varphi[O]$ has compact closure.

Exercise 22 Find a spacetime that is inextendible and hole-free* but not locally inextendible*.

Recall that any spacetime (M, g_{ab}) for which M is compact must be inextendible. Surprisingly, the corresponding claim for local inextendibility* turns out to be false. A counterexample can be constructed by considering an adaptation of ***Misner spacetime*** – a flat, inextendible spacetime that has a cylindrical manifold and light cones that tip over as they move up the cylinder (Misner, 1967). In (t, φ) coordinates, Misner spacetime comes out as $(\mathbb{R} \times S^1, g_{ab})$ where $g_{ab} = 2\nabla_{(a} t \nabla_{b)} \varphi + t \nabla_a \varphi \nabla_b \varphi$ and $0 \leq \varphi \leq 2\pi$. Here, the round brackets indicate the symmetrization operation. In this case, we find that $2\nabla_{(a} t \nabla_{b)} \varphi = \nabla_a t \nabla_b \varphi + \nabla_b t \nabla_a \varphi$ (see Malament, 2012, p. 33). A closed null curve at $t = 0$ is the boundary of the $t > 0$ chronology-violating region in Misner spacetime. A future-incomplete timelike geodesic $\gamma : I \to M$ exists that approaches but never reaches $t = 0$ (see Figure 28).

Let (M, g_{ab}) be the $t < 0$ portion of Misner spacetime in (t, φ) coordinates. One extension to this spacetime is Misner spacetime; let's consider another. The spacetime (M, g_{ab}) can be "reverse twisted" to produce an isometric variant where the light cones tip in the other direction by using the diffeomoprhism $\theta : M \to M$ given by $\theta(t, \varphi) = (t, \varphi + 2\ln(-t))$. This reverse-twisted spacetime can be extended to produce ***reverse Misner spacetime***, which comes out as $(\mathbb{R} \times S^1, g_{ab})$ where $g_{ab} = -2\nabla_{(a} t \nabla_{b)} \varphi + t \nabla_a \varphi \nabla_b \varphi$ and $0 \leq \varphi \leq 2\pi$. We find twisted future-incomplete timelike geodesics in the $t < 0$ portion of Misner spacetime that do not cross $t = 0$ but that can be untwisted and extended

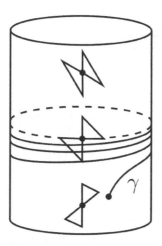

Figure 28 A future-incomplete timelike geodesic γ approaches but never reaches the closed null curve (dotted line).

in reverse Misner spacetime. On the other hand, there are also some twisted future-incomplete timelike geodesics in the $t < 0$ portion of reverse Misner spacetime which do not cross $t = 0$ but that can be untwisted and extended in Misner spacetime. It follows that both Misner and reverse Misner are locally extendible* (cf. Hawking & Ellis, 1973, p. 171). It is not difficult to construct a compact, locally extendible* example that behaves very much like Misner spacetime near $t = 0$. For example, consider the spacetime $(S^1 \times S^1, g_{ab})$ where $g_{ab} = 2\nabla_{(a} t \nabla_{b)} \varphi + \sin(t) \nabla_a \varphi \nabla_b \varphi$ and $0 \le t, \varphi \le 2\pi$ (Beem et al., 1996, p. 244).

The modal "no hole" conditions of inextendibility, local inextendibility*, and hole-freeness* are defined relative to a standard collection of all possible spacetimes. But what is the physical significance of these modal conditions if the standard collection allows for physically unreasonable possibilities? To circumvent the difficulty, one could look for a modal condition to rule out holes that does not depend on a background collection of all possible spacetimes; instead, it would require that regions of a given spacetime are as large as possible in the sense that they are compared to similar regions within the very same model. Here is one example along these lines (cf. Penrose, 1979, p. 623). We say a spacetime (M, g_{ab}) has an ***epistemic hole*** if there is a point $p \in M$ and a pair of future-inextendible timelike geodesics γ and γ' through p such that $\Gamma(\gamma)$ is a proper subset of $\Gamma(\gamma')$ (Manchak, 2016a). In a spacetime with an epistemic hole, two observers are present at the same event and yet one observer eventually has epistemic access to a larger region of spacetime than the other. Clearly, Minkowski spacetime with a point removed has an epistemic hole (see Figure 29).

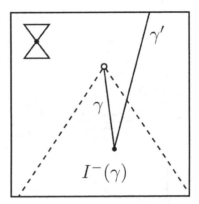

Figure 29 The future-inextendible timelike geodesics γ and γ' have the same past endpoint but since γ approaches the missing point, $\Gamma(\gamma)$ is properly contained in $\Gamma(\gamma')$, which is the entire manifold.

To get a sense of how epistemic hole-freeness relates to other global properties of interest, remove from Minkowski spacetime everything except for the timelike past of a chosen point and apply a conformal factor that goes to infinity as the missing region is approached along every curve. The resulting spacetime will have an epistemic hole despite being globally hyperbolic and geodesically complete. On the other hand, consider time-rolled Minkowski spacetime and remove a point from the manifold; the resulting spacetime counts as epistemically hole-free despite violating chronology, inextendibility, and hole-freeness* (cf. Doboszewski, 2019).

Exercise 23 Find a slice in an epistemically hole-free spacetime with non-empty Cauchy horizon.

How stable are spacetimes with singularities of various kinds? Here is one attempt to get a grip on the question (Geroch, 1969, 1971b). Let $\mathscr{L}(M)$ be the collection of spacetimes with manifold M and let h_{ab} be a positive definite metric on M. At each point in M, the function $d(g_{ab}, g'_{ab}, h_{ab}) = h^{ac}h^{bd}(g_{ab} - g'_{ab})(g_{cd} - g'_{cd})$ assigns a distance between the spacetimes (M, g_{ab}) and (M, g'_{ab}) that can be used to construct various topologies on $\mathscr{L}(M)$. Here, we take a look at two natural possibilities. A $\mathcal{C}$ **neighborhood** of (M, g_{ab}) contains all $(M, g'_{ab}) \in \mathscr{L}(M)$ such that $\text{Sup}_K[d(g_{ab}, g'_{ab}, h_{ab})] < \epsilon$ where h_{ab} is a positive definite metric, $K \subseteq M$ is compact, and $\epsilon > 0$. An $\mathcal{F}$ **neighborhood** of (M, g_{ab}) is defined analogously except the supremum ranges over all of M. These definitions give rise to corresponding $\mathcal{C}$ and $\mathcal{F}$ topologies on $\mathscr{L}(M)$. We say a property of a spacetime (M, g_{ab}) is **stable** relative to a given topology on $\mathscr{L}(M)$ if there is a neighborhood of (M, g_{ab}) in that topology such that every spacetime in the neighborhood also has the property. One can show that chronology is $\mathcal{F}$ stable for a spacetime if and only if the spacetime is stably causal (Hawking & Ellis, 1973, p. 198). We also find that any globally hyperbolic spacetime is $\mathcal{F}$ stable with respect to this property (Beem et al., 1996, p. 242).

In light of the singularity theorems, one might hope to find an appropriate topology to show that large collections of spacetimes are stable with respect to both geodesic incompleteness and some property to rule out physically unreasonable singularities. But neither the $\mathcal{C}$ nor the $\mathcal{F}$ topologies seem appropriate. Consider the $\mathcal{F}$ topology first. It seems to be much too fine since for any spacetime (M, g_{ab}) with non-compact M, the collection of spacetimes $\{(M, \lambda g_{ab})\}$ for $\lambda \in (0, \infty)$ fails to be $\mathcal{F}$ continuous (Geroch, 1971b, p. 71). This suggests that spacetime properties will be too easily counted as $\mathcal{F}$ stable. So it is all the more remarkable that one can construct spacetimes that are $\mathcal{F}$ unstable with respect to geodesic incompleteness (Beem et al., 1996, p. 245). Moreover, one can find spacetimes that are $\mathcal{F}$ unstable with respect to the "no hole" property of local inextendibility* (Manchak, 2018a; cf. Doboszewski, 2020). To see this, start with null-rolled Minkowski spacetime and choose any $\mathcal{F}$ neighborhood around it. The spacetime is locally inextendible* since it is geodesically complete. But the slightest "wiggle" can turn this spacetime into one that is isometric to the locally extendible* Misner spacetime. To get the desired result, one need only smoothly adjust the wiggle so that it goes to zero outside some compact region containing a future-incomplete timelike geodesic (see Figure 30).

Now consider the $\mathcal{C}$ topology. It seems much too coarse since any chronological spacetime whatsoever will be $\mathcal{C}$ unstable with respect to this property (Hawking & Ellis, 1973, p. 198). This suggests that spacetime properties will be be too easily counted as $\mathcal{C}$ unstable. This is confirmed in the cases of geodesic incompleteness and local inextendibility* since the $\mathcal{F}$ instability results above carry over to the present context on account of the fact that any $\mathcal{C}$ neighborhood is a $\mathcal{F}$ neighborhood. And yet some $\mathcal{C}$ stability results are available: any chronology-violating spacetime will be $\mathcal{C}$ stable (and hence $\mathcal{F}$ stable) with respect to this property (Fletcher, 2016).

Exercise 24   Find a spacetime that is $\mathcal{C}$ stable with respect to the property of being inextendible.

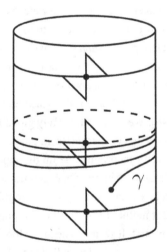

Figure 30 The slightest wiggle of null-rolled Minkowski spacetime can turn it into one that resembles Misner spacetime in the compact region between the top and bottom closed null curves depicted here. The timelike curve γ is a future-incomplete geodesic.

5 Underdetermination

What can we know concerning the global spacetime properties of our own universe? It seems that serious epistemic limitations can arise due to the vast possibilities general relativity affords. We begin by exploring some of the difficulties involved in predicting the global structure of spacetime (Geroch, 1977). Let (M, g_{ab}) be a spacetime with $q \in M$. We say a point $p \in M$ is in the ***domain of prediction*** of q, denoted $P(q)$, if a closed, achronal, spacelike surface $S \subset J^-(q)$ exists such that $p \in D(S) - J^-(q)$. Physically, if S can be observed from q, then a prediction can be made concerning any point $p \in D(S)$ so long as it cannot be observed from q (which would result in a retrodiction instead). Consider space-rolled Minkowski spacetime (M, g_{ab}); since every point q is such that its causal past $J^-(q)$ contains some Cauchy surface, we find that $p \in P(q)$ if and only if $p \notin J^-(q)$ (see Figure 31).

Exercise 25   Find a spacetime (M, g_{ab}) and points $p, q, r \in M$ for which $p \ll q \ll r$ and $P(p) = P(r) = \varnothing$ but $P(q)$ is non-empty.

Now consider Minkowski spacetime (M, g_{ab}) and any closed, achronal, spacelike surface $S \subset M$; if $q \in M$ is such that $S \subset J^-(q)$, we find that $D(S) \subset J^-(q)$, which renders prediction impossible from the point q (see Figure 32). Spacetimes with non-empty domains of prediction turn out to be more the exception than the rule. Indeed, one can show a sense in which future prediction is possible only in a closed universe: if there are points $p, q \in M$ in a spacetime (M, g_{ab})

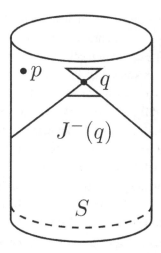

Figure 31 Since the Cauchy surface S is contained in the causal past of the point q, any point p outside of $J^-(q)$ is in the domain of prediction of q.

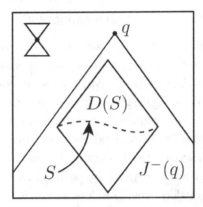

Figure 32 If a closed, achronal, spacelike surface S is contained in the causal past of the point q, then $D(S)$ is also contained in $J^-(q)$.

such that $p \in P(q) \cap I^+(q)$, the spacetime must admit a compact slice (Manchak, 2008). In light of various singularity theorems indicating that a compact slice is sufficient for a physically reasonable spacetime to have singularities, we have a curious corollary here: future prediction is possible in a physically reasonable spacetime only if singularities are present (cf. Hogarth, 1997).

Exercise 26 Define the ***domain of prediction**** to be just as the domain of prediction except drop the requirement that the closed, spacelike surface S must be achronal as well; find a spacetime (M, g_{ab}) with with no compact slice and points $p, q \in M$ such that $p \in P^*(q) \cap I^+(q)$.

Even if a spacetime has a non-empty domain of prediction, it is not clear that prediction is actually possible. Consider again space-rolled Minkowski spacetime. The causal past of each point p contains some Cauchy surface. But how could an observer at p ever know this? If a point to the future of p were missing from the manifold, the surface would no longer be Cauchy and there would be no way of ascertaining this fact from p. Prediction seems to require more than just knowledge about one's past but also knowledge about the entire spacetime into which one's causal past is embedded (Geroch, 1977, p. 86). But one can show various senses in which an observer will generally fail to have the epistemic resources to know the global structure of the spacetime into which her past is embedded. Let us explore this "cosmic underdetermination" subject a bit more (cf. Norton, 2011; Butterfield, 2014).

We say the spacetimes (M, g_{ab}) and (M', g'_{ab}) are ***observationally indistinguishable*** if, for each future-inextendible timelike curve γ in (M, g_{ab}), there is some future-inextendible timelike curve γ' in (M', g'_{ab}) such that $(I^-(\gamma), g_{ab})$

and $(\Gamma(\gamma'), g'_{ab})$ are isometric; and, correspondingly, with the roles of (M, g_{ab}) and (M', g'_{ab}) reversed (Glymour, 1972, 1977). If two spacetimes are observationally indistinguishable, no observer in either spacetime (even one who lives forever) can tell them apart. Consider *de Sitter spacetime* – a model with cylindrical manifold and light cones that close up rapidly as they approach the distant past and future. In (t, x) coordinates, two-dimensional de Sitter spacetime comes out as $(\mathbb{R} \times S^1, g_{ab})$ where $g_{ab} = \nabla_a t \nabla_b t - \cosh^2 t \nabla_a x \nabla_b x$ and $0 \leq x \leq 2\pi$. In this spacetime and its unrolled counterpart, any future-inextendible timelike curve γ has an observational horizon in the sense that $\Gamma(\gamma)$ has a bounded x-width of 2π (see Figure 33). So the two spacetimes are observationally indistinguishable.

Exercise 27 Find an extendible spacetime that is observationally indistinguishable only to itself.

It is not difficult to see that observational indistinguishability is an equivalence relation on the collection of spacetimes. We say a spacetime property is *preserved* under observational indistinguishability if, given any two observationally indistinguishable spacetimes, one has the property if and only if the other does as well. Since observationally indistinguishable spacetimes must be locally isometric, we find that any local property will be preserved under observational indistinguishability. One can also show that various global properties including chronology, causality, and global hyperbolicity are preserved under observational indistinguishability. On the other hand, many other global properties including inextendibility, strong causality, and stable causality are

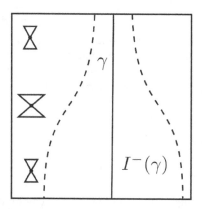

Figure 33 In unrolled de Sitter spacetime, any future-inextendible timelike curve γ is such that its timelike past $\Gamma(\gamma)$ has a bounded x-width of 2π.

not preserved under observational indistinguishability (cf. Malament, 1977a, p. 71). Consider the case of strong causality. Recall that we can construct a space-time violating strong causality if we take time-rolled Minkowski spacetime and delete two well-chosen slits from the manifold. We can unroll this spacetime to produce an observationally indistinguishable counterpart that is strongly causal (see Figure 34).

Consider another example: inextendibility (Malament, 1977a, p. 78). Take two copies of Minkowski spacetime in standard (t, x) coordinates and remove a slit $S = \{(0, x) : 0 \leq x \leq 1\}$ from each copy. Excluding slit boundary points, identify the top edge of S in one copy with the bottom edge of S in the other to produce an inextendible spacetime. To construct an extendible observationally indistinguishable counterpart, just remove the $t \geq 0$ portion in one of the copies (see Figure 35).

Exercise 28   Find a pair of spacetimes showing that hole-freeness* is not preserved under observational indistinguishability.

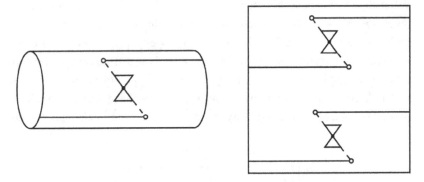

Figure 34 Spacetimes demonstrating that strong causality is not preserved under observational indistinguishability.

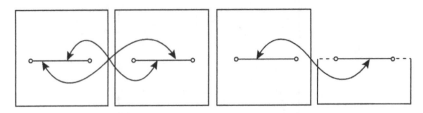

Figure 35 Spacetimes demonstrating that inextendibility is not preserved under observational indistinguishability.

The definition of observational indistinguishability is quite restrictive. We now consider a softened variant (Malament, 1977a, p. 68). Let us say that a spacetime (M, g_{ab}) is **weakly observationally indistinguishable** from a spacetime (M', g'_{ab}) if, for every point $p \in M$, there is a point $p' \in M'$ such that $(\Gamma(p), g_{ab})$ and $(\Gamma(p'), g'_{ab})$ are isometric. The definition is weakened in two senses. First, only observers who do not live forever are considered; one looks at the timelike pasts of points instead of the timelike pasts of future-inextendible timelike curves. Second, the relation is no longer symmetric since the epistemic situation of an observer in one spacetime would seem to be irrelevant to the epistemic situation in another. We find that weak observational indistinguishability is a reflexive, transitive relation on the collection of spacetimes. We see that if two spacetimes are observationally indistinguishable, then either one is weakly observationally indistinguishable from the other. But Minkowski spacetime is weakly observationally indistinguishable from the $t < 0$ portion of Minkowski spacetime and vice versa even though the two spacetimes are not observationally indistinguishable (see Figure 36).

Exercise 29 Find a spacetime (M, g_{ab}) and a point $p \in M$ such that $(M - \{p\}, g_{ab})$ is weakly observationally indistinguishable from (M, g_{ab}) but not the other way around.

As before, we say that a spacetime property is **preserved** under weak observational indistinguishability if, whenever one spacetime is weakly observationally indistinguishable from another, the first has the property only if the second does as well. Because any two observationally indistinguishable

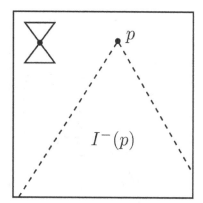
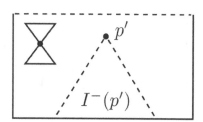

Figure 36 For any point p in Minkowski spacetime and any point p' in the $t < 0$ portion of Minkowski spacetime, the regions $\Gamma(p)$ and $\Gamma(p')$ are isometric.

spacetimes will be such that either spacetime is weakly observationally indistinguishable from the other, we find that any property that is preserved under weak observational indistinguishability will be preserved under observational indistinguishability.

It turns out that one can find examples where a property is preserved under weak observational indistinguishability but not the absence of the property. To see this, consider the case of chronology; global hyperbolicity is very similar (Malament, 1977a, p. 74). If a spacetime has a closed timelike curve, then the curve will be contained in the timelike past of any point on the curve, ensuring that a violation of chronology is preserved under weak observational indistinguishability. On the other hand, consider Minkowski spacetime in standard (t, x) coordinates. Remove two slits $S_n = \{(n, x) : 0 \leq x \leq 1\}$ for $n = 1, 2$ and, excluding the slit boundary points, identify the top edge of each slit with the bottom edge of the other. The resulting spacetime violates chronology since an observer entering S_2 from below must emerge from S_1 from above. Chronology is not preserved under weak observational indistinguishability since Minkowski spacetime is weakly observationally indistinguishable from this chronology-violating spacetime (see Figure 37).

The pair of spacetimes just considered – Minkowski spacetime and its mutilated chronology-violating variant – can be used to show that a number of other spacetime properties are not preserved under weak observational indistinguishability: geodesic completeness, local-inextendibility*, hole-freeness*, and any causal condition between (and including) chronology and global hyperbolicity are just a few examples. The epistemic predicament of the

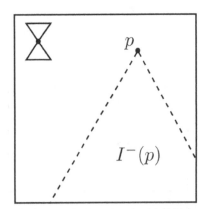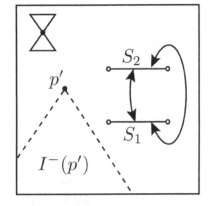

Figure 37 For any point p in Minkowski spacetime, there is a point p' in the depicted chronology-violating spacetime such that the regions $\Gamma(p)$ and $\Gamma(p')$ are isometric.

observer also extends to global properties involving prediction. For example, take space-rolled Minkowski spacetime and cut a slit so that some points have an empty domain of prediction (see Figure 38). This spacetime is constructed so that space-rolled Minkowski spacetime is weakly observationally indistinguishable from it, showing that the property of having a non-empty domain of prediction at every point is not preserved under weak observational indistinguishability.

Exercise 30   Find a spacetime that is weakly observationally indistinguishable from a different (non-isometric) spacetime that is only weakly observationally indistinguishable from itself.

It turns out that only spacetimes with bizarre causal structure do not have a weakly observationally indistinguishable counterpart. Indeed, a counterpart can be found with all of the same local properties as the original in accordance with the demand that "the normal physical laws we determine in our spacetime vicinity are applicable at all other spacetime points" (Ellis, 1975, p. 246). We say that a spacetime (M, g_{ab}) is **causally bizarre** if there is a point $p \in M$ such that $\Gamma(p) = M$. It is immediate that every causally bizarre spacetime violates chronology (but not the other way around). In addition, we find that a spacetime that is totally vicious must be causally bizarre; on the other hand, Misner spacetime is causally bizarre but not totally vicious. Stepping back, one can show that for every spacetime (M, g_{ab}) that is not causally bizarre, there is a spacetime (M', g'_{ab}) such that (i) (M, g_{ab}) and (M', g'_{ab}) are locally isometric

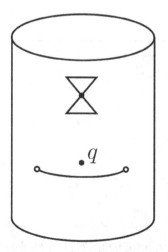

Figure 38 Because of the slit, the point q has an empty domain of prediction.

but not isometric and (ii) (M, g_{ab}) is weakly observationally indistinguishable from (M', g'_{ab}) (Manchak, 2009).

Exercise 31   Find a causally bizarre spacetime that is weakly observationally indistinguishable from a spacetime that is not causally bizarre.

To see why the result must hold, we need to collect a few basic facts. If a spacetime (M, g_{ab}) is not causally bizarre, then for every point $p \in M$, one can find a non-empty open set disjoint from the region $\Gamma^-(p)$. This open set will allow for slits to be cut in M that do not intersect $\Gamma^-(p)$. Another fact we need is this: in every spacetime (M, g_{ab}), there is a countable sequence of points $\{p_n\}$ in M such that $\cup\{\Gamma^-(p_n)\} = M$ (Malament, 1977a, p. 80). It follows that each $q \in M$ will be such that $\Gamma^-(q) \subseteq \Gamma^-(p_n)$ for some point p_n in the sequence. For Minkowski spacetime in standard (t, x) coordinates, the sequence $\{(n, 0)\}$ for $n \in \mathbb{N}$ will have timelike pasts that cover the manifold in this way (see Figure 39).

Now consider any spacetime (M, g_{ab}) that is not causally bizarre and let $\{p_n\}$ be a countable sequence of points in M such that $\cup\{\Gamma^-(p_n)\} = M$. For each $p_n \in M$, consider two copies of the spacetime (M, g_{ab}) – call them (M_n, g_n) and (M'_n, g'_n). In each (M_n, g_n) for $n > 1$, find an open region disjoint from $\Gamma^-(p_n)$ in which to cut a pair of slits S_n^+ and S_n^-; for (M_1, g_1) only cut one slit S_1^+. In each (M'_n, g'_n), cut the slits S_n^+ and S_{n+1}^-. Now, excluding the slit boundary points, identify the top edge of S_1^+ in (M_1, g_1) with the bottom edge of S_1^+ in (M'_1, g'_1); then identify the top edge of S_2^- in (M'_1, g'_1) with the bottom edge of S_2^- in (M_2, g_2); and so on to produce a spacetime chain (M', g'_{ab}) (see Figure 40). It is not difficult to verify that (M, g_{ab}) and (M', g'_{ab}) are locally isometric but

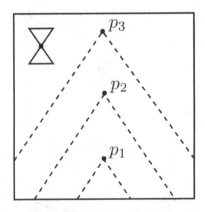

Figure 39 A collection of points $\{p_n\}$ in Minkowski spacetime whose timelike pasts cover the manifold.

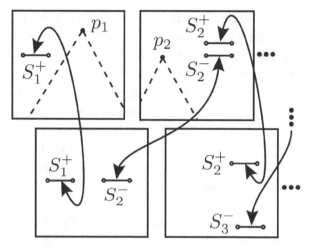

Figure 40 A spacetime chain is produced by identifying slits as indicated.

not isometric and (ii) (M, g_{ab}) is weakly observationally indistinguishable from (M', g'_{ab}).

By removing regions from the weakly observationally indistinguishable counterpart, one can ensure that it fails to satisfy a number of global space-time properties often thought necessary for a physically reasonable spacetime (Manchak, 2011a). In particular, the counterpart can violate the following: causal continuity (and hence causal simplicity and global hyperbolicity) and both inextendibility and hole-freeness* (and hence local inextendibility*). In addition, if one drops the requirement that the weakly observationally indistin-guishable counterpart must be locally isometric to the original, one can ensure that the former even violates chronology (Manchak, 2016b). Stepping back, if all observational evidence we could ever gather (even in principle) is fully consistent with our own universe having "physically unreasonable" properties (even after the local spacetime structure has been fixed in most cases), then perhaps we have been too quick to label these properties as such. In the follow-ing, we build on this line of thought with respect to the property of extendibility.

Exercise 32 Find a collection of spacetimes $\{(M_\lambda, g_\lambda)\}$ for $\lambda \in (0, \infty)$ such that (M_λ, g_λ) is weakly observationally indistinguishable from $(M_{\lambda'}, g_{\lambda'})$ if and only if $\lambda \leq \lambda'$.

6 Extendibility

Here, we explore the modal structure of spacetime through the lens of the inextendibility condition. This is the requirement that spacetime be as large as possible relative to a standard background collection of models. The property is usually taken to be satisfied by all physically reasonable spacetimes for metaphysical reasons (Clarke, 1993, p. 8). "Why, after all, would Nature stop building our universe at M when She could just as well carry on to build M'?" (Geroch, 1970a, p. 262). But inextendibility would seem physically significant only insofar as the background collection coincides with physically reasonable possibilities (Geroch, 1970a, p. 278). Since what counts as a physically reasonable spacetime is not yet clear – especially in light of the aforementioned underdetermination results – one can consider various modified definitions of inextendibility in a pluralistic way.

Let $\mathscr{U}$ be the collection of all spacetimes and let $\mathscr{P} \subseteq \mathscr{U}$ be any spacetime property. If a spacetime is in the collection $\mathscr{P}$, it is a $\mathscr{P}$-***spacetime***. If a $\mathscr{P}$-spacetime is an extension of another $\mathscr{P}$-spacetime, we say the former is a $\mathscr{P}$-***extension*** of the latter. A $\mathscr{P}$-spacetime is $\mathscr{P}$-***extendible*** if it has a $\mathscr{P}$-extension and is $\mathscr{P}$-***inextendible*** otherwise. For all $\mathscr{P} \subseteq \mathscr{U}$, inextendibility implies $\mathscr{P}$-inextendibility although the converse is not true in general. Consider the $t < 0$ portion of Misner spacetime (see Figure 41). It is extendible but counts as $\mathscr{P}$-inextendible if $\mathscr{P}$ is the collection of globally hyperbolic spacetimes (Chrusciel & Isenberg, 1993).

Exercise 33   Find an extendible but $\mathscr{P}$-inextendible spacetime where $\mathscr{P}$ is the collection of all causal spacetimes.

For all spacetime properties $\mathscr{P} \subseteq \mathscr{U}$, consider the following statement.

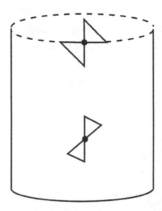

Figure 41 The bottom half of Misner spacetime is extendible and globally hyperbolic, but every extension must fail to be globally hyperbolic.

($*$) Every $\mathscr{P}$-inextendible spacetime is inextendible.

If ($*$) is true for some property $\mathscr{P}$, there is no difference between $\mathscr{P}$-inextendibility and the standard definition. Are there physically reasonable properties $\mathscr{P} \subseteq \mathscr{U}$ that render ($*$) true? Cheap examples abound if one considers various subcollections of the inextendible spacetimes (e.g. the collection of locally inextendible* spacetimes). But ($*$) is usually made false by nontrivial properties. We have seen this in the global hyperbolicity case already. Here is another simple example: take (time and space)-rolled Minkowski spacetime and remove one point from the manifold (see Figure 42). Since the only extension to this spacetime is the one we started with, it counts as $\mathscr{P}$-inextendible where $\mathscr{P}$ is either the collection of all geodesically incomplete spacetimes or the collection of all spacetimes with non-compact manifold. One can also show that ($*$) is false if $\mathscr{P}$ is the collection of all spacetimes satisfying either (i) any of the energy conditions or (ii) any of the causal conditions at least as strong as the causality condition (Manchak, forthcoming). Things are not yet settled with respect to the properties of being non-totally vicious, being chronological, or being vacuum (cf. Geroch, 1970, p. 289).

Exercise 34 Let $\mathscr{P}$ be the collection of all spacetimes that have extendible extensions. Find a spacetime that renders ($*$) false for $\mathscr{P}$.

Because ($*$) is generally false for various physically reasonable properties $\mathscr{P} \subseteq \mathscr{U}$, it seems natural to reexamine foundational claims concerning inextendibility where the standard definition is exchanged for various formulations of $\mathscr{P}$-inextendibility. Recall the result that every extendible spacetime has an inextendible extension; this statement helps to underpin the widely held position that all physically reasonable spacetimes must be inextendible (Earman, 1995, p. 32). But do analogous results hold under variant definitions of

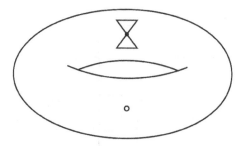

Figure 42 A geodesically incomplete spacetime with non-compact manifold that cannot be extended with these properties but can be extended.

inextendibility? For all spacetime properties $\mathscr{P} \subseteq \mathscr{U}$, consider the following statement.

($**$) Every $\mathscr{P}$-extendible spacetime has a $\mathscr{P}$-inextendible extension.

It is easy to construct physically unreasonable properties that render ($**$) false. Let (M, g_{ab}) be the $t < 0$ portion of Minkowski spacetime in standard (t, x) coordinates and consider the collection $\mathscr{P} = \{(M, g_{ab})\}$. We find that (M, g_{ab}) counts as its own extension; the proper isometric embedding $\varphi : M \to M$ defined by $\varphi(t, x) = (t - 1, x)$ shows this (see Figure 43). So (M, g_{ab}) is $\mathscr{P}$-extendible but it cannot have a $\mathscr{P}$-inextendible extension since (M, g_{ab}) is the only spacetime in $\mathscr{P}$. So ($**$) is false for $\mathscr{P}$.

Exercise 35   Let $\mathscr{P}$ be the collection $\mathscr{U} - \{(M, g_{ab})\}$ where (M, g_{ab}) is Minkowski spacetime. Is ($**$) true or false for $\mathscr{P}$?

What is the status of ($**$) with respect to physically reasonable properties of interest? We find that ($**$) is true if $\mathscr{P}$ is the collection of all chronological spacetimes (Low, 2012). One can also show that ($**$) is also true if $\mathscr{P}$ is the collection of all geodesically incomplete spacetimes. But various physically reasonable subcollections of the geodesically incomplete spacetimes make ($**$) false. For example, take the collection $\mathscr{Q} \subset \mathscr{P}$ of spacetimes such that every maximal timelike geodesic is past-incomplete; presumably, the big bang in our own universe renders $\mathscr{Q}$ physically reasonable in some sense. But one can show that ($**$) is false for $\mathscr{Q}$ (Manchak, 2016c).

Exercise 36   Let $\mathscr{P} \subset \mathscr{U}$ be the collection of geodesically incomplete spacetimes. For each $\mathscr{P}$-extendible spacetime, find a $\mathscr{P}$-inextendible extension.

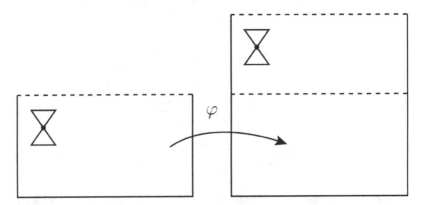

Figure 43 The proper isometric embedding φ shows that the bottom half of Minkowski spacetime counts as its own extension.

To see why this might be, take Minkowski spacetime (M, g_{ab}) in standard (t, x) coordinates and remove the (disjoint) slit $S_n = \{(-n, x) : x \leq -1/n \text{ or } 1/n \leq x\}$ for all positive integers $n \in \mathbb{N}$. Let $S = \cup \{S_n\}$. Consider a conformal factor $\Omega : M - S \to \mathbb{R}$ such that $\Omega = 1$ outside of $D(S)$ but rapidly approaches zero as S is approached along every timelike curve in $D(S)$. We find that the spacetime $(M - S, \Omega^2 g_{ab})$ is inextendible due to the chosen conformal factor. Now remove the points $N = \{(-1, 0), (-2, 0), (-3, 0), \ldots\}$. The result is a $\mathscr{Q}$-spacetime (M', g'_{ab}) since all maximal timelike geodesics must approach either some S_n or some missing point in the past direction (see Figure 44). One can verify that every $\mathscr{Q}$-extension of (M', g'_{ab}) will replace some non-empty subset of N while leaving an infinite number of missing N points. (If only a finite number of missing N points remain in an extension, then a past-complete timelike geodesic running along $x = 0$ can be found to the past of the lowest of the missing N points.) So any extension of (M', g'_{ab}) can itself be $\mathscr{Q}$-extended by replacing any one of the infinite points in N that remain missing in the extension. So (M', g'_{ab}) has no $\mathscr{Q}$-inextendible extension.

One might object that the spacetime just constructed is physically unreasonable in any number of ways. But one employs the cut-and-paste method merely to "demonstrate by some example that a certain assertion is false, or that a certain line of argument cannot work" (Geroch & Horowitz, 1979, p. 221). Here, we see that just because a particular physically reasonable collection $\mathscr{P}$ renders $(**)$ true, it does not follow that every physically reasonable subcollection $\mathscr{Q} \subset \mathscr{P}$ will render $(**)$ true as well; each collection must be checked independently. And even if one considers extremely nice spacetime properties, one still needs to worry about their various subcollections. Take the collection of

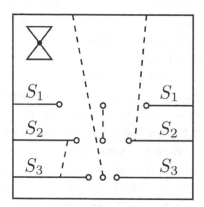

Figure 44 All maximal timelike geodesics (dotted lines) are past-incomplete since each one must approach either some S_n or some missing point.

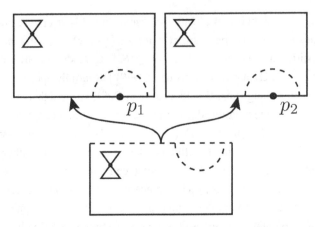

Figure 45 The points p_1 and p_2 are distinct, but open neighborhoods around these points will always intersect in the bottom half of the spacetime.

globally hyperbolic spacetimes; simply being a member of this collection is not sufficient to be considered physically reasonable even if one goes along with the controversial "cosmic censorship" position that all physically reasonable spacetimes must be globally hyperbolic.

So far, we have only considered $\mathscr{P}$-inextendibility in cases where $\mathscr{P} \subseteq \mathscr{U}$. It is also fruitful to study $\mathscr{P}$-inextendibility for various collections of geometric objects $\mathscr{P}$ for which $\mathscr{U}$ is a subcollection. For example, one could allow for spacetimes with continuous but non-smooth metrics (Galloway & Ling, 2017; Sbierski, 2018). Let $\mathscr{V}$ be the collection of spacetimes (M, g_{ab}) that are defined as before except that M is now permitted to be non-Hausdorff (Hájíček, 1971a, 1971b). As before, a member of $\mathscr{P} \subseteq \mathscr{V}$ will be called a $\mathscr{P}$-*spacetime*. In the natural way, one can also extend the definitions of various $\mathscr{P}$-extendibility notions to include all $\mathscr{P} \subseteq \mathscr{V}$. A simple example of a $(\mathscr{V} - \mathscr{U})$-spacetime is constructed by considering two copies of Minkowski spacetime in standard (t, x) coordinates. Identify each point (t, x) in one copy with the point (t, x) in the other copy if and only if $t < 0$; the result is $\mathscr{V}$-spacetime in which Minkowski spacetime "branches" at $t = 0$. Since the points $p_1 = (0, 0)$ and $p_2 = (0, 0)$ in each of the copies are not identified, these points are distinct in the branching model. But open neighborhoods around these points must intersect in the $t < 0$ region, demonstrating that the spacetime is non-Hausdorff (see Figure 45). In the natural way, we can also extend the scope of $(**)$ to apply to all $\mathscr{P} \subseteq \mathscr{V}$. Because there is no limit to the number of non-Hausdorff branches that can be attached to a $\mathscr{V}$-spacetime, $(**)$ comes out as false for $\mathscr{V}$ (Clarke, 1976, p. 18).

Exercise 37   For any $(M, g_{ab}) \in \mathscr{U}$ that is not causally bizarre, find a $(\mathscr{V} - \mathscr{U})$-spacetime (M', g'_{ab}) such that (i) (M, g_{ab}) and (M', g'_{ab}) are locally isometric but not isometric and (ii) (M, g_{ab}) is weakly observationally indistinguishable from (M', g'_{ab}).

Consider Misner spacetime (M, g_{ab}) in (t, φ) coordinates. Recall that a future-incomplete timelike geodesic spirals around the spacetime and never reaches $t = 0$. This geodesic can be extended beyond $t = 0$ if one "reverse twists" the $t < 0$ portion of (M, g_{ab}) and then extends to produce reverse Misner spacetime (M', g'_{ab}). But then a different geodesic will become twisted in reverse Misner spacetime and fail to reach $t = 0$. It turns out that one can combine the two variants of Misner spacetime so as to extend both geodesics across $t = 0$ if one allows for non-Hausdorff possibilities (Hawking & Ellis, 1973, p. 173). Let (N, g_{ab}) and (N', g'_{ab}) be, respectively, the $t < 0$ portions of Misner and reverse Misner and let $\theta : N \to N'$ be the reverse twist isometry. A non-Hausdorff branching Misner spacetime (M'', g''_{ab}) can be constructed by considering the spacetimes (M, g_{ab}) and (M', g'_{ab}) and identifying each point $(t, \varphi) \in N \subset M$ with the point $\theta(t, \varphi) \in N' \subset M'$ (see Figure 46).

Despite being non-Hausdorff, the branching Misner spacetime seems physically reasonable in a number of ways (Geroch, 1968b, p. 240). We say that a $\mathscr{V}$-spacetime (M, g_{ab}) has **bifurcating curves** if there exist curves $\gamma_n : [0, 1] \to M$ for $n = 1, 2$ and some $t \in (0, 1]$ such that $\gamma_1(s) = \gamma_2(s)$ for all $s < t$ and yet $\gamma_1(s) \neq \gamma_2(s)$ for all $s \geq t$. Immediately, we find that the branching Minkowski spacetime has bifucating curves. In each copy (M_n, g_n) of Minkowski spacetime for $n = 1, 2$ consider the curve $\gamma_n : [0, 1] \to M_n$ defined

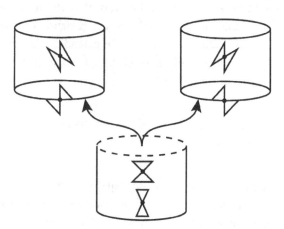

Figure 46 A non-Hausdorff branching version of Misner spacetime; the bottom half is symmetrically depicted here.

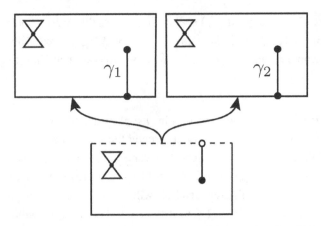

Figure 47 The branching version of Minkowski spacetime has bifurcating curves since γ_1 and γ_2 coincide only when $t < 0$.

by $\gamma_n(s) = (-1 + 2s, 0)$. When the $t < 0$ regions of (M_1, g_1) and (M_2, g_2) are identified to produce the branching Minkowski spacetime, we find that $\gamma_1(s) = \gamma_2(s)$ for all $s < 1/2$ but $\gamma_1(s) \neq \gamma_2(s)$ for all $s \geq 1/2$ (see Figure 47).

It turns out that the branching Misner spacetime is curiously free of bifurcating curves (cf. Hájíček, 1971a). Moreover, we find the collection $\mathscr{W}$ of $\mathscr{V}$-spacetimes without bifurcating curves is also nice in the following ways: (i) every $\mathscr{W}$-spacetime has an underlying manifold that is second countable, (ii) every strongly causal $\mathscr{W}$-spacetime is a $\mathscr{U}$-spacetime (i.e. it is Hausdorff), and (iii) one can show (using Zorn's lemma) that $\mathscr{W}$ renders $(\ast\ast)$ true (Clarke, 1976). Result (iii) ensures that the $t < 0$ portion of Misner spacetime has a $\mathscr{W}$-inextendible extension that, although non-Hausdorff, can be considered the "natural extension" (Geroch, 1968c, p. 465). Result (iii) is also useful in pushing back against the position that any non-Hausdorff spacetime must be physically unreasonable since it must be extendible in the sense that it can be properly and isometrically embedded it into some other non-Hausdorff spacetime (cf. Earman, 2008, p. 202).

Exercise 38 Find a collection $\mathscr{P} \subset \mathscr{V}$ that renders $(\ast\ast)$ true and contains $\mathscr{W}$ as a proper subcollection.

Let (M, g_{ab}) be the $t < 0$ portion of Misner spacetime in (t, φ) coordinates and let $\mathscr{P} \subseteq \mathscr{V}$ be any collection containing this spacetime. We find that demanding $\mathscr{P}$-inextendibilty can often "force" (M, g_{ab}) to have extensions with particular global properties (Earman et al., 2009). For example, if $\mathscr{P} = \mathscr{U}$, then every

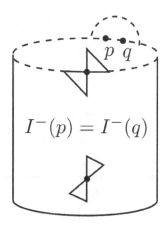

Figure 48 Every extension to the bottom half of Misner spacetime contains a pair of distinct points p and q such that $\Gamma^-(p) = \Gamma^-(q)$.

$\mathscr{P}$-inextendible $\mathscr{P}$-extension of (M, g_{ab}) fails to be distinguishing (see Figure 48). If $\mathscr{P} = \mathscr{W}$, then every $\mathscr{P}$-inextendible $\mathscr{P}$-extension of (M, g_{ab}) is non-Hausdorff (cf. Hawking & Ellis, 1973, p. 174). And so on. We find that once $\mathscr{P}$ is fixed, we can think of (M, g_{ab}) as a type of machine that forces various global properties of interest. Let's explore this idea a bit more (cf. Earman et al., 2016).

We say a $\mathscr{P}$-spacetime (M, g_{ab}) for $\mathscr{P} \subseteq \mathscr{V}$ is $\mathscr{P}$-*past-inextendible* if, for every isometric embedding $\varphi : M \to M'$ into a $\mathscr{P}$-spacetime (M', g'_{ab}), we have $\Gamma^-(\varphi[M]) = \varphi[M]$. A $\mathscr{P}$-spacetime (M, g_{ab}) for $\mathscr{P} \subseteq \mathscr{V}$ is a $\mathscr{P}$-*starter* if it is globally hyperbolic and $\mathscr{P}$-past-inextendible, and has a $\mathscr{P}$-inextendible extension. A $\mathscr{P}$-starter represents a universe with a physically reasonable property that has future extensions that are as large as possible with the property. Under this definition, the $t < 0$ portion of Misner spacetime counts as a $\mathscr{U}$-starter and a $\mathscr{W}$-starter, but not a $\mathscr{V}$-starter given that it fails to be $\mathscr{V}$-past-inextendible.

For all $\mathscr{P}, \mathscr{Q} \subseteq \mathscr{V}$, a $\mathscr{P}$-starter is a $(\mathscr{P}, \mathscr{Q})$-*machine* if all of its $\mathscr{P}$-inextendible extensions are $\mathscr{Q}$-extensions. If $\mathscr{P}$ is a collection of physically reasonable spacetimes, then a $(\mathscr{P}, \mathscr{Q})$-machine represents a physically reasonable universe that forces the property $\mathscr{Q}$ to obtain. (One usually considers nontrivial $(\mathscr{P}, \mathscr{Q})$-machines in which the $\mathscr{P}$-starter lacks the property $\mathscr{Q}$.) For example, let $\mathscr{T} \subset \mathscr{U}$ be the collection of chronology-violating spacetimes; a $(\mathscr{P}, \mathscr{T})$-machine can be considered a type of time machine relative to the collection $\mathscr{P} \subseteq \mathscr{V}$. A remarkable result shows that a $(\mathscr{U}, \mathscr{T})$-machine does not exist where $\mathscr{U}$ is the collection of Hausdorff spacetimes (Krasnikov, 2002, 2018). In the case of the $t < 0$ portion of Misner spacetime (M, g_{ab}), a chronological $\mathscr{U}$-extension can be constructed by taking Misner spacetime (M', g'_{ab})

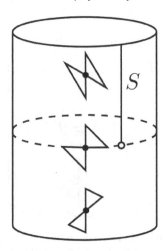

Figure 49 The removed slit S does not permit closed timelike curves.

in (t, φ) coordinates with the slit $S = \{(t, 0) : t \geq 0\}$ removed (see Figure 49). Of course, the spacetime $(M' - S, g_{ab})$ is $\mathscr{U}$-extendible. But one can introduce a conformal factor $\Omega : M' - S \rightarrow \mathbb{R}$ such that $\Omega = 1$ in the $t < 0$ region of $M' - S$ but rapidly approaches zero as S is approached along every curve contained in the $t > 0$ region. So the resulting spacetime $(M' - S, \Omega^2 g_{ab})$ is a chronological $\mathscr{U}$-inextendible extension of (M, g_{ab}).

Exercise 39 Find a chronological, flat, $\mathscr{U}$-inextendible extension of the $t < 0$ portion of Misner spacetime.

Are there physically reasonable collections $\mathscr{P} \subset \mathscr{U}$ such that a $(\mathscr{P}, \mathscr{T})$-machine exists? It has been suggested that if $\mathscr{P}$ is a property forbidding holes of some kind, perhaps such a time machine existence result can be found (Earman et al., 2009). Indeed, it has even been claimed that if $\mathscr{P}$ is the collection of causally closed spacetimes, then a $(\mathscr{P}, \mathscr{T})$-machine exists (Manchak, 2011b). But this claim turns out to be false. To see why, consider the following no-go result. Let $\mathscr{R} \subset \mathscr{U}$ be the collection of reflecting spacetimes. Let $\mathscr{P} \subseteq \mathscr{R}$ be any subcollection of reflecting spacetimes (e.g. the collection of causally closed spacetimes) and suppose a $(\mathscr{P}, \mathscr{T})$-machine (M, g_{ab}) exists. It follows that (M, g_{ab}) has a $\mathscr{P}$-inextendible extension (M', g'_{ab}) that violates chronology. It is not hard to verify that (M', g'_{ab}) cannot be totally vicious. (To see this, suppose (M', g'_{ab}) is totally vicious. Let $\varphi : M \rightarrow M'$ be the proper isometric embedding of (M, g_{ab}) into (M', g'_{ab}). Consider $\varphi(p)$ for any point $p \in M$. Since (M', g'_{ab}) is totally vicious, recall that $\Gamma^-(\varphi(p)) = M'$ (Minguzzi, 2019, p. 113).

It follows that $\Gamma(\varphi[M]) = M' \neq \varphi[M]$, which is impossible since (M, g_{ab}) is a $\mathscr{P}$-starter and hence $\mathscr{P}$-past-inextendible. Since (M', g'_{ab}) both violates chronology and is not totally vicious, recall that it must fail to be reflecting (Clarke & Joshi, 1988), which is impossible since (M', g'_{ab}) is a $\mathscr{P}$-spacetime. So we find that no $(\mathscr{P}, \mathscr{T})$-machine exists where $\mathscr{P} \subseteq \mathscr{R}$. It remains to be seen whether other physically reasonable collections $\mathscr{P} \subset \mathscr{U}$ can yield a time machine existence result.

In contrast to the time machine case, we find a number of available "hole machine" existence results; here is one such (Manchak, 2014b). Let $\mathscr{H} \subset \mathscr{U}$ be the collection of spacetimes with holes in the sense that they fail to be causally closed, and let $\mathscr{E} \subset \mathscr{U}$ be the collection of empty (i.e. vacuum) spacetimes. In three or more dimensions, it is not difficult to see that an $(\mathscr{E}, \mathscr{H})$-machine must exist. Consider the $t < 0$ portion of three-dimensional Misner space-time (M, g_{ab}) (see Chrusciel & Isenberg, 1993). Because (M, g_{ab}) is flat and $\mathscr{U}$-past-inextendible, it must be $\mathscr{E}$-past-inextendible. Since (M, g_{ab}) is also globally hyperbolic and has Misner spacetime as an extension (which is flat and inextendible and therefore $\mathscr{E}$-inextendible), it counts as an $\mathscr{E}$-starter. Let (M', g'_{ab}) be any $\mathscr{E}$-inextendible extension to (M, g_{ab}). By the argument given in the previous paragraph, we see that if (M', g'_{ab}) were totally vicious, then (M, g_{ab}) would fail to be $\mathscr{E}$-past-inextendible, which is impossible; so (M', g'_{ab}) is not totally vicious. But since (M', g'_{ab}) is not totally vicious and at least three-dimensional, it is causally closed if and only if it is causally simple (Hounnonkpe & Minguzzi, 2019). Because every extension to the $t < 0$ portion of Misner spacetime – including (M', g'_{ab}) – fails to be distinguishing, we know that (M', g'_{ab}) must fail to be causally simple. So (M', g'_{ab}) must fail to be causally closed as well.

Exercise 40   Find a two-dimensional $(\mathscr{E}, \mathscr{H})$-machine.

Let us take a look at one final machine example. Let $\mathscr{M} \subset \mathscr{U}$ be the collection of Malament-Hogarth spacetimes. One can show that a $(\mathscr{U}, \mathscr{M})$-machine must exist (Manchak, 2018b). To see this, consider Minkowski spacetime (M, g_{ab}) in standard (t, x) coordinates. Let $q = (0, 0)$ and let $C = J^+(q)$. Now consider the spacetime $(M - \{q\}, \Omega^2 g_{ab})$ where $\Omega : M - \{q\} \to \mathbb{R}$ is chosen to go to infinity as the missing point q is approached along any curve. Let (M', g'_{ab}) be the spacetime $(M - C, \Omega^2 g_{ab})$. This spacetime contains a past-extendible timelike curve $\gamma : I \to M'$ that approaches the missing point q and is such that $\|\gamma\| = \infty$ due to the chosen conformal factor. We find that the spacetime (M', g'_{ab}) is globally hyperbolic and counts as a $\mathscr{U}$-starter. Let (M'', g''_{ab}) be any $\mathscr{U}$-inextendible extension of (M', g'_{ab}). One can verify that for any point

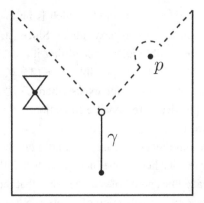

Figure 50 The past-extendible timelike curve γ approaching the missing
point has infinite length but is contained in the timelike past of the point p.

$p \in M'' - M'$ on the boundary of M' in M'', the region $\Gamma(p)$ will contain the
image of the curve γ (see Figure 50). So (M'', g''_{ab}) is Malament-Hogarth and
(M', g'_{ab}) counts as a $(\mathcal{U}, \mathcal{M})$-machine The example fails to have a nice local
structure and so one naturally wonders about the existence of other $(\mathcal{P}, \mathcal{M})$-
machines for various choices of physically reasonable properties $\mathcal{P} \subset \mathcal{U}$.

Appendix

The appendix comes in two parts. In the first, there is a brief review of some basic topology (Steen & Seebach, 1970; Wald, 1984). In the second, sample solutions to all exercises are presented.

Topology Basics

In what follows, let $\mathbb{R}$, $\mathbb{Q}$, $\mathbb{Z}$, and $\mathbb{N}$ be, respectively, the set of real numbers, rational numbers, integers, and positive integers. A ***topological space*** $(X, \mathcal{T})$ consists of a set X and a collection $\mathcal{T}$ of subsets of X satisfying (i) $\varnothing, X \in \mathcal{T}$, (ii) if $O_\alpha \in \mathcal{T}$ for all α, then $\bigcup_\alpha O_\alpha \in \mathcal{T}$, and (iii) if $O_1, \ldots, O_n \in \mathcal{T}$, then $\bigcap_{i=1}^n O_i \in \mathcal{T}$. If $(X, \mathcal{T})$ is a topological space, then $\mathcal{T}$ is a ***topology*** on X. A set $O \subseteq X$ is ***open*** if $O \in \mathcal{T}$. A set $C \subseteq X$ is ***closed*** if $X - C$ is open. A set $A \subseteq X$ is a ***neighborhood*** of $p \in X$ if there is an open set $O \subseteq A$ such that $p \in O$. For any set X, the collection $\{A : A \subseteq X\}$ is the ***discrete*** topology on X while the collection $\{\varnothing, X\}$ is the ***indiscrete*** topology on X. Consider the topological space $(\mathbb{R}, \mathcal{T})$ where $\mathcal{T}$ is a collection of all sets $O \subseteq \mathbb{R}$ where O can be expressed as a union of open intervals $(a, b) = \{x \in \mathbb{R} : a < x < b\}$. This is the standard topology on $\mathbb{R}$. We see, for example, that the disjoint region $\mathbb{R} - \{0\}$ is open, the interval $[0, 1] = \{x \in \mathbb{R} : 0 \le x \le 1\}$ is closed, and the interval $(-1, 1] = \{x \in \mathbb{R} : -1 < x \le 1\}$ is neither open nor closed but does count as a neighborhood of 0.

If $(X_1, \mathcal{T}_1)$ and $(X_2, \mathcal{T}_2)$ are topological spaces, the ***product*** topology on $X_1 \times X_2$ is the collection of all subsets of $X_1 \times X_2$, which can be expressed as unions of sets of the form $O_1 \times O_2$ with $O_1 \in \mathcal{T}_1$ and $O_2 \in \mathcal{T}_2$. The standard topology on $\mathbb{R}$ can be used to define the product topology on $\mathbb{R} \times \mathbb{R} = \mathbb{R}^2$. The construction can be repeated to define a topology on $\mathbb{R}^n$ for any $n \in \mathbb{N}$. This is the ***standard*** topology on $\mathbb{R}^n$ and it is assumed unless otherwise noted. Consider the ***open ball*** $B_\epsilon(p) \subset \mathbb{R}^n$ with radius $\epsilon > 0$ centered at the point $p = (p_1, \ldots, p_n) \in \mathbb{R}^n$, which is defined as the set of all points $(x_1, \ldots, x_n) \in \mathbb{R}^n$ such that $(\sum_{i=1}^n (p_i - x_i)^2)^{1/2} < \epsilon$ (see Figure 51). If $\mathcal{T}$ is the collection of sets $O \subseteq \mathbb{R}^n$ such that, for all $p \in O$, there is an $\epsilon > 0$ with $B_\epsilon(p) \subset O$, we find that $\mathcal{T}$ is the standard topology on $\mathbb{R}^n$.

If $\mathcal{T}_1$ and $\mathcal{T}_2$ are topologies on X and $\mathcal{T}_1 \subset \mathcal{T}_2$, then $\mathcal{T}_1$ is more ***coarse*** than $\mathcal{T}_2$ and $\mathcal{T}_2$ is more ***fine*** than $\mathcal{T}_1$. For any topological space $(X, \mathcal{T})$ and any $A \subseteq X$, the ***closure*** of A, denoted $\mathrm{cl}(A)$, is the intersection of all closed sets containing A; the ***interior*** of A, denoted $\mathrm{int}(A)$, is the union of all open sets contained in A; the ***boundary*** A, denoted $\mathrm{bd}(A)$ is the set $\mathrm{cl}(A) - \mathrm{int}(A)$. The

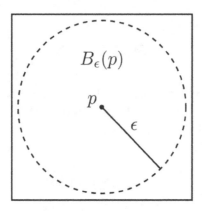

Figure 51 The ball $B_\epsilon(p)$ in $\mathbb{R}^2$ with radius ϵ centered at the point p.

following are true: (i) $\text{cl}(A)$ is closed, $A \subseteq \text{cl}(A)$, and $A = \text{cl}(A)$ if A is closed; (ii) $\text{int}(A)$ is open, $\text{int}(A) \subseteq A$, and $A = \text{int}(A)$ if A is open; (iii) $\text{bd}(A)$ is closed and $\text{cl}(A) = \text{int}(A) \cup \text{bd}(A)$. As a simple example, consider the set $A = (-1, 1]$ in $\mathbb{R}$. We find that $\text{cl}(A) = \{-1\} \cup A$, $\text{int}(A) = A - \{1\}$, and $\text{bd}(A) = \{-1, 1\}$. A set $A \subseteq X$ is **dense** in the topological space $(X, \mathcal{T})$ if $\text{cl}(A) = X$. The sets $\mathbb{Q}$ and $\mathbb{R} - \mathbb{Q}$ are both dense in $\mathbb{R}$.

For any topological space $(X, \mathcal{T})$ and any $A \subseteq X$, the collection $\mathcal{T}_{|A} = \{U : U = A \cap O, O \in \mathcal{T}\}$ is the **induced** topology on A. For all $n \in \mathbb{N}$, the n-sphere S^n is the set $\{(x_1, \ldots, x_{n+1}) \in \mathbb{R}^{n+1} : \sum_{i=1}^{n+1} x_i^2 = 1\}$. The **standard** topology on S^n – which is assumed throughout – is the induced topology from $\mathbb{R}^{n+1}$. Let $(X, \mathcal{T})$ be a topological space and let $\sim$ be some equivalence relation on X. Consider the quotient set $Y = X/\sim$ defined as $\{[x] : x \in X\}$ where $[x] = \{y \in X : x \sim y\}$ is the equivalence class of x. Let $f : X \to Y$ be the function $f(x) = [x]$. The **quotient topology** on Y is the collection $\{O \subseteq Y : f^{-1}[O] \in \mathcal{T}\}$. To see the definition at work, let X be the closed interval $[0, 1]$ with induced topology from $\mathbb{R}$. Now consider the quotient set $Y = X/\sim$ where, for all $x, y \in X$, we have $x \sim y$ if and only if (i) $x = y$, or (ii) $x = 0$ and $y = 1$, or (iii) $x = 1$ and $y = 0$. One finds that Y with the quotient topology is homeomorphic to S^1. A similar construction shows how the entire real line can be rolled up into a circle. Just let $Y = \mathbb{R}/\sim$ where, for all $x, y \in \mathbb{R}$, we have $x \sim y$ if and only if $x - y \in \mathbb{Z}$; the set Y with the quotient topology is homeomorphic to S^1.

If $(X, \mathcal{T})$ and $(Y, \mathcal{S})$ are topological spaces, a function $f : X \to Y$ is **continuous** if, for every open set $O \subseteq Y$, the set $f^{-1}[O] = \{x \in X : f(x) \in O\}$ is open in X. Consider the function $f : \mathbb{R} \to \mathbb{R}^2$ defined by $f(x) = (x, -1)$ for $x \neq 0$ and $f(0) = (0, 1)$. We find that f is not continuous since the open set $O = \{(x, y) : y > 0\}$ in $\mathbb{R}^2$ is such that $f^{-1}[O] = \{0\}$, which is not open in $\mathbb{R}$ (see Figure 52). The topological spaces $(X, \mathcal{T})$ and $(Y, \mathcal{S})$ are **homeomorphic** if there is a bijection $f : X \to Y$ such that f and its inverse f^{-1} are

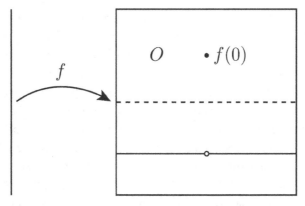

Figure 52 The function $f: \mathbb{R} \to \mathbb{R}^2$ is not continuous since the open set O in $\mathbb{R}^2$ is such that $f^{-1}[O] = \{0\}$ is not open in $\mathbb{R}$.

continuous. Topological spaces that are homeomorphic have all of the same topological properties. We find that $\mathbb{R}$ is homeomorphic to the interval $(-1, 1)$ with induced topology from $\mathbb{R}$ since the bijection $f: (-1, 1) \to \mathbb{R}$ given by $f(x) = \tan(\pi x/2)$ is continuous and so is its inverse. For additional examples, consider (i) the cylinder $\mathbb{R} \times S^1$ with the product topology, (ii) the once punctured plane $\mathbb{R}^2 - \{(0,0)\}$ with induced topology from $\mathbb{R}^2$, and (iii) the twice punctured sphere $S^2 - \{(1,0,0), (-1,0,0)\}$ with induced topology from S^2; each of these topological spaces is homeomorphic to any other.

A topological space $(X, \mathscr{T})$ is **connected** if the only subsets of X that are both open and closed are $\varnothing$ and X itself. A topological space $(X, \mathscr{T})$ is **path connected** if, for all $p, q \in X$, there is a continuous function $f: [0, 1] \to X$ such that $f(0) = p$ and $f(1) = q$. We find $\mathbb{R}^n$ and S^n are path connected for all $n \in \mathbb{N}$. One can show that every path connected topological space is connected but the converse is false. One counterexample is the "topologist's sine curve" $(X, \mathscr{T})$ where $X = \{(x, \sin(1/x)) \in \mathbb{R}^2 : x > 0\} \cup \{(0,0)\}$ and $\mathscr{T}$ is the induced topology from $\mathbb{R}^2$. A topological space $(X, \mathscr{T})$ is **Hausdorff** if, for any distinct $p, q \in X$, there are disjoint open sets $U, V \subset X$ such that $p \in U$ and $q \in V$. One can verify that $\mathbb{R}^n$ and S^n are Hausdorff for all $n \in \mathbb{N}$. If $(X, \mathscr{T})$ and $(Y, \mathscr{S})$ are Hausdorff topological spaces, then (i) any $A \subset X$ with the induced topology is Hausdorff and (ii) $X \times Y$ with the product topology is Hausdorff. The "line with two origins" is an example of a non-Hausdorff topological space. Consider the set $\{1, 2\}$ with the discrete topology and let $X = \mathbb{R} \times \{1, 2\}$ have the product topology. Let $\sim$ be an equivalence relation on X where, for all $x, y \in \mathbb{R}$ and all $n, m \in \{1, 2\}$, we have $(x, n) \sim (y, m)$ if and only if either $(x, n) = (y, m)$ or $x = y \neq 0$. The set $X/\sim$ with the quotient topology is not Hausdorff since any open sets around the two origin points $(0, 1)$ and $(0, 2)$ must intersect.

Let $(X, \mathscr{T})$ be a topological space with $p, q \in X$. Let $\gamma : [0, 1] \to X$ and $\gamma' : [0, 1] \to X$ be continuous curves with $\gamma(0) = \gamma'(0) = p$ and $\gamma(1) = \gamma'(1) = q$. The curves γ and γ' are **homotopic** if there is a continuous function $h : [0, 1] \times [0, 1] \to X$ such that $h(0, s) = \gamma(s)$ and $h(1, s) = \gamma'(s)$ for all $s \in [0, 1]$ and $h(t, 0) = p$ and $h(t, 1) = q$ for all $t \in [0, 1]$. Homotopic curves are those that can be continuously deformed into one another while keeping the endpoints fixed. A topological space $(X, \mathscr{T})$ is **simply connected** if it is path-connected and every continuous curve $\gamma : [0, 1] \to X$ for which $\gamma(0) = \gamma(1)$ is homotopic to the trivial curve $\gamma' : [0, 1] \to X$ for which $\gamma'(s) = \gamma(0)$ for all $s \in [0, 1]$. One can show that $\mathbb{R}^n$ is simply connected for all $n \in \mathbb{N}$ and S^n is simply connected if and only if $n \geq 2$. In the case of S^1, the continuous curve $\gamma : [0, 1] \to S^1$ defined by $\gamma(s) = (\cos(2\pi s), \sin(2\pi s))$ that loops around S^1 is not homotopic to the trivial curve $\gamma' : [0, 1] \to S^1$ defined by $\gamma'(s) = \gamma(0) = (1, 0)$ (see Figure 53).

Let $(X, \mathscr{T})$ be a topological space. The topological space $(Y, \mathscr{S})$ is a **covering space** of $(X, \mathscr{T})$ if there is map $f : Y \to X$ (called the **covering map**) that satisfies the following condition: for each $x \in X$, there is an open set $O \subset X$ containing x such that $f^{-1}[O]$ is a disjoint union of sets, each of which is mapped homeomorphically onto O by f. Any topological space counts as its own covering space. If a covering space $(Y, \mathscr{S})$ of $(X, \mathscr{T})$ is simply connected, then $(Y, \mathscr{S})$ is a **universal covering space** of $(X, \mathscr{T})$. Intuitively, if there are any non-homotopic curves in a topological space, its universal covering space unwinds them. If $(Y, \mathscr{S})$ is a universal covering space of $(X, \mathscr{T})$, then it is a covering space of all other connected covering spaces of $(X, \mathscr{T})$. Given any topological space, one can show that any two of its universal covering spaces

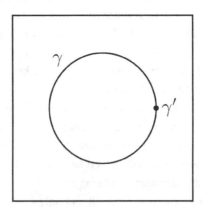

Figure 53 Because the curve γ loops around S^1, it is not homotopic to the trivial curve γ' at the point $\gamma(0)$.

are homeomorphic. We see that $\mathbb{R}^n$ is its own universal covering space for all $n \in \mathbb{N}$ and S^n is its own universal covering space if and only if $n \geq 2$. The universal covering space of S^1 is $\mathbb{R}$; the covering map $f: \mathbb{R} \to S^1$ defined by $f(x) = (\cos(2\pi x), \sin(2\pi x))$ can be used to show this.

If $(X, \mathcal{T})$ is a topological space and $A \subseteq X$, a collection $\{O_\alpha\}$ of open sets is an **open cover** for A if the union of all of the sets in the collection contains A. Any subcollection of the sets $\{O_\alpha\}$ that also cover A is a **subcover**. The set A is **compact** if every open cover of A has a finite subcover. The open interval $(0, 1)$ in $\mathbb{R}$ is not compact since the open sets $O_n = (1/(n + 1), 1)$ for $n \in \mathbb{N}$ give rise to an open cover for $(0, 1)$, which fails to have a finite subcover. We find that S^n is compact and $\mathbb{R}^n$ is not compact for all $n \in \mathbb{N}$. In $\mathbb{R}^n$, one can show that a set A is compact if and only if it is closed and bounded in the sense that A is contained in the open ball $B_\epsilon(p)$ for some $\epsilon > 0$ and some $p \in \mathbb{R}^n$ (see Figure 54). If $(X, \mathcal{T})$ is a Hausdorff topological space, the following are true: (i) if $A \subseteq X$ is compact, then A is closed; (ii) if X is compact and $A \subseteq X$ is closed, then A is compact; (iii) if $A \subseteq X$ is compact, then for any continuous function $f: A \to \mathbb{R}$, there exist $a, b \in \mathbb{R}$ such that, for all $x \in A$, $a \leq f(x) \leq b$ with $f(p) = a$ and $f(q) = b$ for some $p, q \in A$. We also find that if $(X, \mathcal{T})$ and $(Y, \mathcal{S})$ are compact topological spaces, then the space $X \times Y$ is compact in the product topology. So, for example, the torus $S^1 \times S^1$ is compact.

The set $\mathcal{B} \subseteq \mathcal{T}$ is a **basis** for the topological space $(X, \mathcal{T})$ if every open set $O \in \mathcal{T}$ can be expressed as a union of sets in $\mathcal{B}$. A topological space $(X, \mathcal{T})$ is **second countable** if there is a countable basis for it. We find that $\mathbb{R}^n$ and S^n are second countable for all $n \in \mathbb{N}$. In the case of $\mathbb{R}^n$, a countable basis can be found by taking the collection of all open balls $B_\epsilon(p)$ where $\epsilon \in \mathbb{Q}$ and

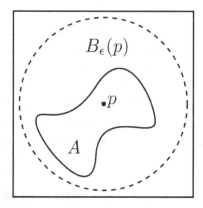

Figure 54 The closed set $A \subset \mathbb{R}^2$ is compact since it is contained in the open ball $B_\epsilon(p)$ for some $\epsilon > 0$ and some $p \in \mathbb{R}^2$.

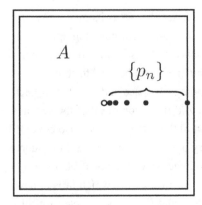

Figure 55 The closed set $A \subset X$ is not compact since the sequence $\{p_n\}$ in A
fails to have an accumulation point in A.

$p = (p_1, \ldots, p_n)$ is such that $p_1, \ldots, p_n \in \mathbb{Q}$. For a simple example of topological
space that fails to be second countable, consider $(\mathbb{R}, \mathscr{T})$ where $\mathscr{T}$ is the discrete
topology. If $(X, \mathscr{T})$ is a topological space, a point $p \in X$ is an ***accumulation
point*** of an infinite sequence $\{p_n\}$ in X if every open neighborhood of p contains
infinitely many points in the sequence. In $\mathbb{R}$, the sequence $\{p_n\}$ defined by
$p_n = (n/n+1)(-1)^n$ for all $n \in \mathbb{N}$ has accumulation points at -1 and 1. A useful
result is the following: if a topological space $(X, \mathscr{T})$ is second countable, then
a set $A \subseteq X$ is compact if and only if every infinite sequence $\{p_n\}$ in A has
an accumulation point p in A. Consider $X = \mathbb{R}^2 - \{(0,0)\}$ with the induced
topology from $\mathbb{R}^2$ and the closed set $A = \{(x_1, x_2) \in X : -1 \leq x_n \leq 1$ for $n = 1, 2\}$. We see that $A \subset X$ is not compact since the sequence $\{p_n\}$ in A defined
by $p_n = (1/n, 0)$ for all $n \in \mathbb{N}$ has no accumulation point at all, let alone one in
A (see Figure 55).

Let $(X, \mathscr{T})$ be a topological space and let $\{O_\alpha\}$ be an open cover of X.
An open cover $\{V_\beta\}$ is a ***refinement*** of $\{O_\alpha\}$ if for each V_β there is an O_α
such that $V_\beta \subset O_\alpha$. A cover $\{V_\beta\}$ is ***locally finite*** if each $x \in X$ has an
open neighborhood W such that only finitely many V_β satisfy $W \cap V_\beta \neq \emptyset$.
A topological space $(X, \mathscr{T})$ is ***paracompact*** if every open cover $\{O_\alpha\}$ has
a locally finite refinement $\{V_\beta\}$. One can show that $\mathbb{R}^n$ and S^n are paracompact for all $n \in \mathbb{N}$. In addition, any compact topological space is paracompact.
To construct a topological space that is not paracompact, take $(\mathbb{R}, \mathscr{T})$ where
$\mathscr{T} = \{O \subseteq \mathbb{R} : 0 \in O\} \cup \{\emptyset\}$.

A topological space $(M, \mathscr{T})$ is a (topological) ***manifold*** of dimension $n \in \mathbb{N}$
if each point $p \in M$ has an open neighborhood $O \subset M$ such that O with
the induced topology and $\mathbb{R}^n$ are homeomorphic. Intuitively, a n-dimensional

manifold has a topology that is locally like that of $\mathbb{R}^n$. The topological spaces $\mathbb{R}^n$ and S^n are manifolds for any dimension $n \in \mathbb{N}$. Consider, for example, the point $p = (1,0,0) \in S^2$; the set $O = \{(x,y,z) \in S^2 : x > 0\}$ is an open neighborhood of p which is homeomorphic to $\mathbb{R}^2$. If M is an n-dimensional manifold and $C \subset M$ is a closed proper subset, then $M - C$ with the induced topology is an n-dimensional manifold. If M and N are, respectively, m-dimensional and n-dimensional manifolds, then $M \times N$ with the product topology is an $(m + n)$-dimensional manifold. A useful result is this: any connected Hausdorff manifold is paracompact if and only if it second countable. A manifold of dimension $n \geq 4$ can fail to be smooth in the appropriate sense, but $\mathbb{R}^n$ and S^n are smooth for any dimension $n \in \mathbb{N}$.

Sample Solutions

Sample solutions to all exercises are presented here; familiarity with all definitions given in the preceding is assumed.

Exercise 1   Find a manifold M and a point $p \in M$ such that M and $M - \{p\}$ are diffeomorphic.

Let M be the manifold $\mathbb{R}^2$ with the closed set of points $\{(n,0)\}$ removed for all positive integers $n \in \mathbb{N}$ and take $p = (0,0)$. The bijection $\varphi : M \to M - \{p\}$ given by $\varphi(x,y) = (x-1,y)$ is a diffeomorphism (cf. Geroch & Horowitz, 1979, p. 289).

Exercise 2   Find a spacetime (M, g_{ab}) and a pair of points $p, q \in M$ that can be connected by spacelike and null geodesics but not by a timelike geodesic.

Consider space-rolled Minkowski spacetime (M, g_{ab}) in (t, φ) coordinates. The pair of points $p = (0,0)$ and $q = (2\pi, 0)$ can be connected by timelike, null, and spacelike geodesics. But if the point $(1, 0)$ is removed, the resulting spacetime is such that p and q fail to be connected by a timelike geodesic (see Figure 56).

Exercise 3   Find a flat spacetime such that every maximal timelike geodesic is incomplete but some maximal null and spacelike geodesics are complete.

Consider Minkowski spacetime (M, g_{ab}) and any point $p \in M$. The spacetime $(M - J^+(p), g_{ab})$ will be such that every maximal timelike geodesic will approach the missing region while some maximal spacelike and null geodesics can avoid it.

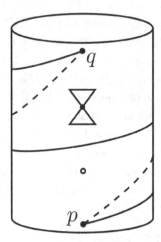

Figure 56 The points p and q can be connected by a spacelike geodesic (solid line) and a null geodesic (dotted line) but not by a timelike geodesic due to the missing point.

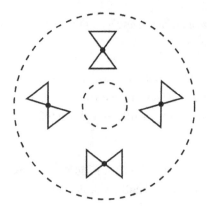

Figure 57 The annulus with rotating light cones does not admit a continuous timelike vector field.

Exercise 4 Find a spacetime (M, g_{ab}) for some $M \subset \mathbb{R}^2$ that fails to be time-orientable.

Delete a closed set of points from $\mathbb{R}^2$ to leave an open annulus; orient the light cones so they rotate around the annulus (see Figure 57). The resulting spacetime is not time-orientable (cf. Geroch & Horowitz, 1979, p. 227).

Exercise 5 Find a spacelike surface in Minkowski spacetime that fails to be achronal.

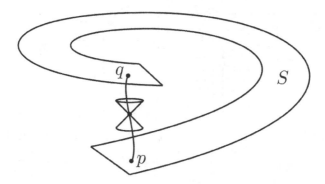

Figure 58 A "spiraling ramp" spacelike surface S in three-dimensional Minkowski spacetime is such that the points p and q in S can be connected by a timelike curve.

An example in two-dimensional Minkowski spacetime does not exist. But a "spiraling ramp" spacelike surface can be found in three three-dimensional Minkowski spacetime such that two points in the surface can be connected by a timelike curve (see Figure 58).

Exercise 6 Find a pair of non-isometric spacetimes such that each counts as an extension of the other.

Consider two copies of the $t < 0$ portion of Minkowski spacetime in standard (t, x) coordinates. Remove one point from the manifold of one copy. The resulting spacetimes are not isometric but each counts as an extension of the other (cf. Geroch, 1970, p. 276).

Exercise 7 Find a flat, inextendible spacetime $(\mathbb{R}^2, g_{ab})$ that is not isometric to Minkowski spacetime.

For each $n \in \mathbb{Z}$, let (M_n, g_n) be a copy of Minkowski spacetime in standard (t, x) coordinates. In each (M_n, g_n) delete the slit $S_n = \{(t, 0) : t \geq 0\}$. Excluding the origin point in each copy, identify the right edge of the slit S_n in (M_n, g_n) with the left edge of the slit S_{n+1} in (M_{n+1}, g_{n+1}) for all $n \in \mathbb{Z}$ to produce a flat, inextendible spacetime (see Figure 59). Because of the missing origin points, the resulting spacetime is geodesically incomplete and therefore not isometric to Minkowski spacetime. But one can verify that the underlying manifold is the universal covering space of $\mathbb{R}^2 - \{(0, 0)\}$, which is just $\mathbb{R}^2$ (see Geroch & Horowitz, 1979, p. 232).

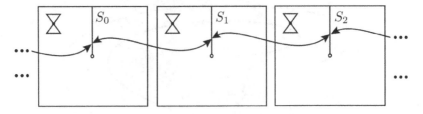

Figure 59 The right edge of the slit S_n in (M_n, g_n) is identified with the left edge of the slit S_{n+1} in (M_{n+1}, g_{n+1}) for all $n \in \mathbb{Z}$.

Exercise 8 Is being time-orientable a global property? Is being two-dimensional?

Consider two-dimensional Minkowski spacetime (M, g_{ab}) in standard (t, x) coordinates and remove from M all points for which $|x| > 1$. Now, identify the point $(t, 1)$ with the point $(-t, -1)$ for all t to produce a flat spacetime that is not time-orientable. Because the resulting spacetime is locally isometric to Minkowski spacetime, we find that time-orientability is a global property. Because spacetimes can be locally isometric only if they share the same dimension, we find being two-dimensional counts as a local property.

Exercise 9 Find a spacetime (M, g_{ab}) and points $p, q \in M$ such that $p \ll p$, $q \ll q$, and $p \ll q$ but $q \not\ll p$.

Consider $(S^1 \times S^1, g_{ab})$ where $g_{ab} = 2 \cos \varphi \nabla_{(a} \varphi \nabla_{b)} t + \sin^2 \varphi (\nabla_a t \nabla_b t - \nabla_a \varphi \nabla_b \varphi)$ and $0 \leq t, \varphi \leq 2\pi$. The light cones are oriented so that the closed causal curves at $\varphi = \pi/2$ and $\varphi = 3\pi/2$ are timelike. But the closed causal curves at $\varphi = 0$ and $\varphi = \pi$ are null and the light cones tip in different directions along these closed null curves (Malament, 1977a, p. 78). We find that any pair of points $p = (t, \varphi)$ and $q = (t', \varphi')$ will have the desired properties if $\pi < \varphi < 2\pi$ and $0 < \varphi' < \pi$ (see Figure 60).

Exercise 10 Find a geodesically complete spacetime (M, g_{ab}) and a point $p \in M$ such that $J^-(p)$ is not closed.

Consider Minkowski spacetime (M, g_{ab}) in standard (t, x) coordinates. Remove the origin $q = (0, 0)$ from M and then construct the conformally equivalent spacetime $(M - \{q\}, \Omega^2 g_{ab})$ where $\Omega : M - \{q\} \to \mathbb{R}$ goes to infinity as the missing point q is approached along any curve. The resulting spacetime is geodesically complete due to the chosen conformal factor, but it must have

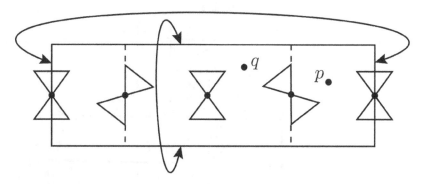

Figure 60 Each of the points p and q can be connected to itself via a future-directed timelike curve; in addition, there is a future-directed timelike curve from p to q but not the other way around.

the same causal structure as Minkowski spacetime with the origin removed. In particular, the point $p = (1, 1)$ will be such that $J^-(p)$ is not closed.

Exercise 11 Find a causal spacetime (M, g_{ab}) and a discontinuous bijection $\theta : M \to M$ such that for all $p, q \in M$, $p \ll q$ if and only if $\theta(p) \ll \theta(q)$.

Consider the spacetime $(\mathbb{R} \times S^1, g_{ab})$ where $g_{ab} = 2\nabla_{(a}t\nabla_{b)}\varphi + \sinh^2 t \nabla_a\varphi\nabla_b\varphi$ and $0 \leq \varphi \leq 2\pi$. The light cones tip over as they move from the distant past to form a single closed null curve at $t = 0$ at which point they tip back as they move into the distant future. Now remove the slits $S_1 = \{(t, 0) : t \geq 0\}$ and $S_2 = \{(t, \pi) : t \geq 0\}$ and let (M, g_{ab}) be the resulting causal but not distinguishing spacetime (see Figure 61). Consider the discontinuous bijection $\theta : M \to M$ where $\theta(t, \varphi) = (t, \varphi)$ for $t < 0$ and $\theta(t, \varphi) = (t, \varphi + \pi)$ for $t \geq 0$. We find that for all $p, q \in M$, $p \ll q$ if and only if $\theta(p) \ll \theta(q)$ (Malament, 2012, p. 135).

Exercise 12 Find a spacetime that satisfies strong causality but violates stable causality.

Consider time-rolled Minkowski spacetime in (t, x) coordinates. Remove the slits $S_1 = \{(0, x) : 0 \leq x\}$, $S_2 = \{(1, x) : x \leq 1\}$, and $S_3 = \{(2, x) : 0 \leq x\}$ (see Figure 62). We find that strong causality is satisfied, but closed timelike curves form if the light cones are opened by a small amount at each point (Hawking & Ellis, 1973, p. 197).

Exercise 13 Find a spacetime that satisfies stable causality but violates causal continuity.

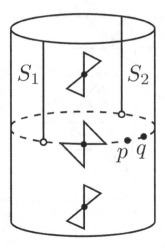

Figure 61 Due to the removed slits S_1 and S_2, the spacetime is causal. But the timelike pasts of the distinct points p and q coincide (the region below the dotted line).

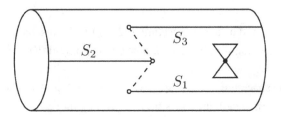

Figure 62 The removed slits S_1, S_2, and S_3 are chosen so that the spacetime is strongly causal but not stably causal.

Consider Minkowski spacetime (M, g_{ab}) in standard (t, x) coordinates and remove the slit $S = \{(0, x) : 0 \leq x\}$. The resulting spacetime $(M-S, g_{ab})$ inherits a global time function from Minkowski spacetime. But consider the points $p = (1, 1)$ and $q = (-1, -1)$; we find that $I^+(p) \subset I^+(q)$ but $I^-(q) \not\subset I^-(p)$ showing that causal continuity does not hold (cf. Hawking & Sachs, 1974, p. 289).

Exercise 14   Find a Malament-Hogarth spacetime that is flat and satisfies chronology.

Let (M, g_{ab}) and (M', g'_{ab}) be two copies of Minkowski spacetime in standard (t, x) coordinates. Define a past-extendible timelike curve $\gamma : (0, \infty) \to M$ with infinite length by setting $\gamma(s) = (s, -1)$. Now for each $n \in \mathbb{N}$, remove the slit $S_n = \{(n, x) : 0 \leq x \leq 1\}$ from (M, g_{ab}) and the slit $S'_n = \{(-n, x) : 0 \leq x \leq 1\}$

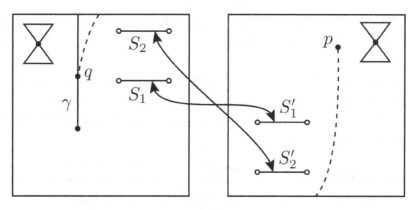

Figure 63 There is a future-directed timelike curve (dotted line) from each point q on the curve γ that enters one of the slits S_n from below and emerges from the slit S'_n from above to reach the point p.

from (M', g'_{ab}). Identify the bottom edge of the slit S_n with the top edge of the slit S'_n for all $n \in \mathbb{N}$ and let the resulting flat spacetime be (M'', g''_{ab}). We find that any point $p \in M''$ from which there is a past-directed timelike curve meeting the top edge of each slit S'_n will be such that its timelike past includes the image of γ, which shows (M'', g''_{ab}) to be Malament-Hogarth (see Figure 63). But one can verify that the spacetime contains no closed timelike curves.

Exercise 15 In Minkowski spacetime (M, g_{ab}), find slices $S, S' \subset M$ such that $D(S) \cap D(S') = \varnothing$ but $D(S) \cup D(S') = M$.

Consider Minkowski spacetime (M, g_{ab}) in standard (t, x) coordinates. Let the slice $S \subset M$ be the union of $S_1 = \{(1, x) : x \leq 0\}$ and $S_2 = \{(t, x) : t = (x^2 + 1)^{1/2}, x > 0\}$; we find that $D(S)$ is the region $t > x$. Let the slice $S' \subset M$ be the union of $S'_1 = \{(t, x) : t = x, x \leq 0\}$ and $S'_2 = \{(0, x) : x > 0\}$; we find that $D(S')$ is the region $t \leq x$. So $D(S) \cap D(S') = \varnothing$ and $D(S) \cup D(S') = M$.

Exercise 16 Find a manifold M that admits a Lorentzian metric but is such that every spacetime (M, g_{ab}) fails to have a Cauchy surface.

Let M be the manifold $\mathbb{R}^2$ with two distinct points removed. Since it is non-compact, it admits a Lorentzian metric. But since there is no $N \subset M$ such that M is homeomorphic to $\mathbb{R} \times N$, we find that any spacetime (M, g_{ab}) must fail to be globally hyperbolic (cf. Geroch & Horowitz, 1979, p. 252).

Exercise 17 Find a spacetime that satisfies the strong energy condition but violates the weak energy condition.

Consider a four-dimensional version of de Sitter spacetime for which $R = 32\pi$. We find that $T_{ab} = -g_{ab}$ showing that the weak energy condition must be violated. Since $T = T^a{}_a = -n = -4$, we have $T_{ab} - \frac{1}{2}Tg_{ab} = g_{ab}$, showing that the strong energy condition is satisfied.

Exercise 18 Find a four-dimensional, stably causal spacetime with compact slice that satisfies the strong energy condition but is geodesically complete.

Consider a four-dimensional version of space-rolled Minkowski spacetime where each t =constant surface is a compact slice of topology $S^1 \times S^1 \times S^1$. The spacetime is flat (and thus satisfies the strong energy condition), globally hyperbolic (and thus stably causal), and yet geodesically complete.

Exercise 19 Find a causally simple spacetime with detectable naked singularity.

Take Minkowski spacetime (M, g_{ab}) in standard (t, x) coordinates and remove all points for which $|x| \geq 1$. The spacetime is causally simple, but the image of a future-incomplete timelike geodesic approaching $x = 1$ will be contained in the timelike past of some point p (see Figure 64).

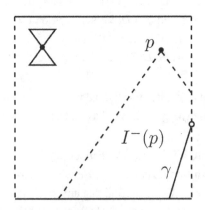

Figure 64 The point p is such that the region $I^-(p)$ contains the future-incomplete timelike geodesic γ.

Exercise 20 Find a spacetime with detectable naked singularity but no evolved naked singularity; find a spacetime with an evolved naked singularity but no detectable naked singularity.

Time-rolled Minkowski spacetime with a point removed has a detectable naked singularity but admits no slice and is therefore free of evolved naked singularities. Now consider Minkowski spacetime with a point removed and a conformal factor applied that goes to infinity as the missing point is approached along every curve. The result is a geodesically complete spacetime (and so must be free of detectable naked singularities), but since it has the same same causal structure as Minkowski spacetime with a point removed, it must have evolved naked singularities.

Exercise 21 Find an inextendible, causally continuous spacetime that is not hole-free*.

Consider Minkowski spacetime (M, g_{ab}) in standard (t, x) coordinates and let $O = I^+(p)$ for $p = (0, 0)$. Remove p from M and then construct the conformally equivalent spacetime $(M - \{p\}, \Omega^2 g_{ab})$ where $\Omega : M - \{p\} \to \mathbb{R}$ is such that (i) $\Omega = 1$ for all points outside of O and (ii) goes to zero as the missing point p is approached along any curve contained in O. The resulting spacetime is inextendible due to the chosen conformal factor. It has the same causal structure as Minkowski spacetime with a point removed; in particular, it is causally continuous. But the slice $S = \{(t, x) : t = -1\}$ is such that $D(S)$ is open and the spacetime $(D(S), g_{ab})$ is globally hyperbolic. We find that $(D(S), g_{ab})$ does not effectively extend itself. But since $\Omega = 1$ on $D(S)$, there is an isometric embedding $\varphi : D(S) \to M$ into Minkowski spacetime (M, g_{ab}) such that $\varphi[D(S)]$ is a proper subset of the interior of $D(\varphi[S])$ and $\varphi[S]$ is achronal (see Figure 65). So $(D(S), g_{ab})$ has an effective extension and $(M - \{p\}, \Omega^2 g_{ab})$ is not hole-free*.

Exercise 22 Find a spacetime that is inextendible and hole-free* but not locally inextendible*.

Consider Minkowski spacetime (M, g_{ab}) in standard (t, x) coordinates and let $O = I^-(p)$ for $p = (0, 0)$. Remove the region $C = \{(t, x) : t \geq 0\}$ from M and then construct the conformally equivalent spacetime $(M - C, \Omega^2 g_{ab})$ where $\Omega : M - C \to \mathbb{R}$ is such that (i) $\Omega = 1$ for all points in O and (ii) goes to infinity as the missing region C is approached along any curve outside of O. The resulting spacetime is inextendible due to the chosen conformal factor. It

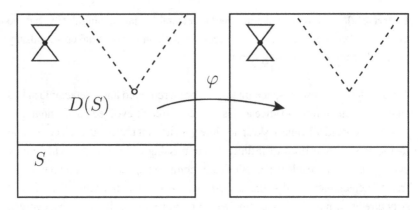

Figure 65 The slice S is such that the globally hyperbolic region $D(S)$ can be effectively extended by isometrically embedding it via φ into Minkowski spacetime.

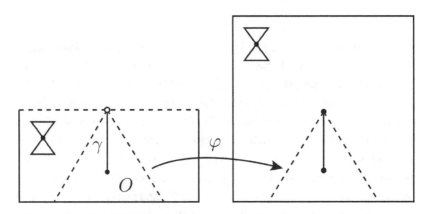

Figure 66 An open set O containing the future-incomplete timelike geodesic γ can be isometrically embedded via φ into Minkowski spacetime such that $\varphi \circ \gamma$ has past and future endpoints.

has the same causal structure as the $t < 0$ portion of Minkowski spacetime and so must be globally hyperbolic. These facts together ensure that the spacetime is also hole-free*. But the curve $\gamma : (0, 1) \to O$ defined by $\gamma(s) = (s - 1, 0)$ is a past-extendible future-incomplete timelike geodesic that approaches the missing point p. Since $\Omega = 1$ on O, there is an isometric embedding $\varphi : O \to M$ into Minkowski spacetime (M, g_{ab}) such that the curve $\varphi \circ \gamma$ has a past and future endpoints (see Figure 66). This means that $(M - C, \Omega^2 g_{ab})$ is locally extendible*.

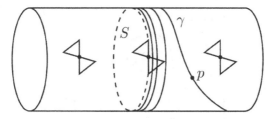

Figure 67 The point p is not in the domain of dependence of the slice S since the inextendible timelike curve γ approaches but never never meets S.

Exercise 23 Find a slice in an epistemically hole-free spacetime with non-empty Cauchy horizon.

Consider null-rolled Minkowski spacetime (M, g_{ab}). Each closed null curve $S \subset M$ counts as a slice. But we find that $D(S) = S$ and therefore $H(S) = S$ since, through any point $p \in M - S$, there will be an inextendible timelike curve that fails to meet S (see Figure 67). But one can verify that the timelike past of any future-inextendible timelike geodesic will be all of M.

Exercise 24 Find a spacetime that is C stable with respect to the property of being inextendible.

Let (M, g_{ab}) be any spacetime for which M is compact. Since each member of the collection $\mathscr{L}(M)$ is compact, each member must also be inextendible. So inextendibility is C stable for any spacetime in $\mathscr{L}(M)$.

Exercise 25 Find a spacetime (M, g_{ab}) and points $p, q, r \in M$ for which $p \ll q \ll r$ and $P(p) = P(r) = \varnothing$ but $P(q)$ is non-empty.

Consider Minkowski spacetime (M, g_{ab}) in standard (t, x) coordinates and remove the slits $S_1 = \{(-2, x) : -1 \le x \le 1\}$ and $S_2 = \{(2, x) : -1 \le x \le 1\}$. Excluding boundary points, identify the bottom edge of S_1 with the top edge of S_2. In the resulting spacetime, there is a closed, achronal, spacelike surface S contained in the region $\mathscr{J}^-(q)$ for the point $q = (0, 0)$ such that $D(S)$ extends outside of $\mathscr{J}^-(q)$ (see Figure 68). So the domain of predication of q in not empty. But points to the distant past and future of q that can be reached by timelike curves going around the slits will have empty domains of prediction (cf. Geroch, 1977, p. 90).

Exercise 26 Define the ***domain of prediction**** to be just as the domain of prediction except drop the requirement that the closed, spacelike surface S must

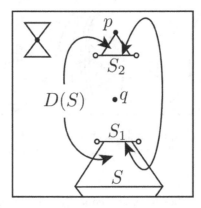

Figure 68 The closed, achronal, spacelike surface S is contained in the causal past of the point q. But since $D(S)$ extends outside of the causal past of q, there is a point p in the domain of predication of q.

be achronal as well; find a spacetime (M, g_{ab}) with no compact slice and points $p, q \in M$ such that $p \in P^*(q) \cap I^+(q)$.

Consider Minkowski spacetime (M, g_{ab}) in standard (t, x) coordinates and remove the slits $S_1 = \{(1, x) : -4 \leq x \leq -3\}$, $S_2 = \{(1, x) : 3 \leq x \leq 4\}$, $S_3 = \{(-1, x) : -2 \leq x \leq -1\}$, and $S_4 = \{(-1, x) : 1 \leq x \leq 2\}$. Excluding boundary points, identify the bottom edge of S_1 with the top edge of S_3 and the top edge of S_4 with the bottom edge of S_2. The resulting spacetime (M', g'_{ab}) admits no compact slice (cf. Hogarth, 1993, p. 726). But one can find a point $q \in M'$ for which $J^-(q)$ contains a closed, spacelike surface S such that $D(S)$ extends outside of outside of $J^-(q)$ and into the region $I^+(q)$ (see Figure 69). So there is a point p in $P^*(q) \cap I^+(q)$.

Exercise 27   Find an extendible spacetime that is observationally indistinguishable only to itself.

First note that Minkowski spacetime (M, g_{ab}) is only observationally indistinguishable to itself. To see why, consider a future-inextendible timelike curve γ such that $I^-(\gamma) = M$; any observationally indistinguishable counterpart (M', g'_{ab}) must either be isometric to (M, g_{ab}) or extend (M, g_{ab}), but the latter possibility can be ruled out since Minkowski spacetime is inextendible. Now remove a point $p \in M$ from Minkowski spacetime (M, g_{ab}). The resulting spacetime (M', g'_{ab}) is extendible and will have a future-inextendible timelike curve γ' such that $I^-(\gamma') = M'$. So any observationally indistinguishable counterpart must either be isometric to (M', g'_{ab}) or extend (M', g'_{ab}). The latter possibility

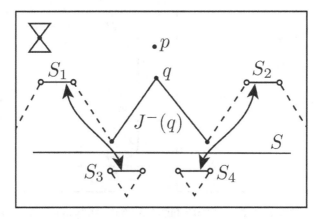

Figure 69 The point q is such that the closed, spacelike surface S is contained in $J^-(q)$. But the point $p \in I^+(q)$ is in $D(S)$ but not $J^-(q)$.

can be ruled out since the only extension to (M', g'_{ab}) is Minkowski spacetime, which is only observationally indistinguishable from itself.

Exercise 28 Find a pair spacetimes showing that hole-freeness* is not preserved under observational indistinguishability.

Let (M, g_{ab}) be the $t < 0$ portion of Minkowski spacetime; it is not hole-free* since it can be effectively extended in Minkowski spacetime. Now consider the spacetime $(\Gamma(p), g_{ab})$ for any point $p \in M$; it is hole-free*. But one can verify that the two spacetimes are observationally indistinguishable.

Exercise 29 Find a spacetime (M, g_{ab}) and a point $p \in M$ such that $(M - \{p\}, g_{ab})$ is weakly observationally indistinguishable from (M, g_{ab}) but not the other way around.

Let (M, g_{ab}) be the unrolled de Sitter spacetime in (t, x) coordinates with the points $(0, 0)$, $(0, 2\pi)$, and $(1, 2\pi)$ removed. If $p = (1, 0)$ we find that the spacetime $(M - \{p\}, g_{ab})$ is weakly observationally indistinguishable from (M, g_{ab}). But the timelike past of the point $q = (2, 0)$ in (M, g_{ab}) has no isometric counterpart in $(M - \{p\}, g_{ab})$ (see Figure 70); so (M, g_{ab}) is not weakly observationally indistinguishable from $(M - \{p\}, g_{ab})$.

Exercise 30 Find a spacetime that is weakly observationally indistinguishable from a different (non-isometric) spacetime that is only weakly observationally indistinguishable from itself.

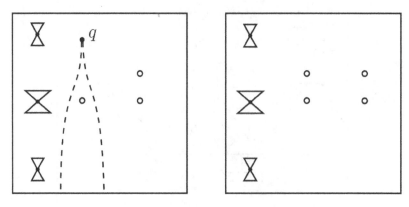

Figure 70 The timelike past of q fails have have an isometric counterpart in the spacetime with the extra missing point.

If (M, g_{ab}) is the $t < 0$ portion of Misner spacetime and (M', g'_{ab}) is Misner spacetime, it is immediate that the former is weakly observationally indistinguishable from the latter. But $\Gamma^-(p) = M'$ for any point $p \in M'$ in the $t > 0$ portion of Misner spacetime (M', g'_{ab}). It follows that because Misner spacetime is inextendible, it can only be weakly observationally indistinguishable from itself.

Exercise 31 Find a causally bizarre spacetime that is weakly observationally indistinguishable from a spacetime that is not causally bizarre.

Consider the spacetime (M, g_{ab}) where $M = S^1 \times S^1$ and $g_{ab} = 2\cos\varphi\nabla_{(a}\varphi\nabla_{b)}t + \sin^2\varphi(\nabla_a t\nabla_b t - \nabla_a\varphi\nabla_b\varphi)$ and $0 \le t, \varphi \le 2\pi$. The light cones are oriented so that the closed causal curves at $\varphi = \pi/2$ and $\varphi = 3\pi/2$ are timelike. But the closed causal curves at $\varphi = 0$ and $\varphi = \pi$ are null and the light cones tip in different directions along these closed null curves (recall Figure 60). Remove all points (t, φ) for which $0 \le \varphi \le \pi$ and let the resulting spacetime be (M', g'_{ab}). We find that any point $p \in M'$ is such that $\Gamma^-(p) = M'$; so (M', g'_{ab}) is causally bizarre (see Figure 71). Now construct a spacetime (M'', g''_{ab}) that is not causally bizarre by unrolling (M, g_{ab}) along the φ direction (cf. Malament, 1977a, p. 78). One can verify that (M', g'_{ab}) is weakly observationally indistinguishable from (M'', g''_{ab}).

Exercise 32 Find a collection of spacetimes $\{(M_\lambda, g_\lambda)\}$ for $\lambda \in (0, \infty)$ such that (M_λ, g_λ) is weakly observationally indistinguishable from $(M_{\lambda'}, g_{\lambda'})$ if and only if $\lambda \le \lambda'$.

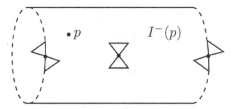

Figure 71 The spacetime is causally bizarre since the timelike past of any point p is the entire manifold.

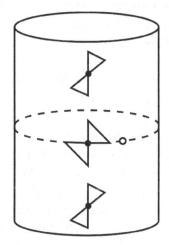

Figure 72 Because of the missing point, the spacetime is both extendible and causal.

For each $\lambda \in (0, \infty)$, let (M_λ, g_λ) be the $0 < t < \lambda$ portion of Minkowski spacetime in standard (t, x) coordinates. One can verify that (M_λ, g_λ) is weakly observationally indistinguishable from $(M_{\lambda'}, g_{\lambda'})$ if and only if $\lambda \leq \lambda'$.

Exercise 33 Find an extendible but $\mathscr{P}$-inextendible spacetime where $\mathscr{P}$ is the collection of all causal spacetimes.

Consider the spacetime (M, g_{ab}) where $M = \mathbb{R} \times S^1$ and $g_{ab} = 2\nabla_{(a}t\nabla_{b)}\varphi - \sinh^2 t \nabla_a \varphi \nabla_b \varphi$ with $0 \leq \varphi \leq 2\pi$. The light cones tip over as they move from the distant past to form a single closed null curve at $t = 0$ at which point they tip back as they move into the distant future (see Malament, 2012, p. 135). Now remove a point $p = (0, 0)$ from the closed null curve to produce an extendible spacetime that satisfies causality (see Figure 72). But this spacetime has only one extension: the causality violating (M, g_{ab}). So $(M - \{p\}, g_{ab})$ is $\mathscr{P}$-inextendible where $\mathscr{P} \subset \mathscr{U}$ is the collection of causal spacetimes.

Exercise 34   Let $\mathscr{P}$ be the collection of all spacetimes that have extendible extensions. Find a spacetime that renders $(*)$ false for $\mathscr{P}$.

Let $\mathscr{P}$ be the collection of all spacetimes that have extendible extensions. For any distinct points $p, q \in M$ in Minkowski spacetime (M, g_{ab}), consider the spacetime $(M - \{p, q\}, g_{ab})$. It has an extendible extension – the spacetime $(M - \{p\}, g_{ab})$ for example. So $(M - \{p, q\}, g_{ab})$ is a $\mathscr{P}$-spacetime. But every extension of $(M - \{p, q\}, g_{ab})$ is either Minkowski spacetime (which is inextendible) or Minkowski spacetime with one point removed (which can only be extended to the inextendible Minkowski spacetime). So the extendible $(M - \{p, q\}, g_{ab})$ is $\mathscr{P}$-inextendible.

Exercise 35   Let $\mathscr{P}$ be the collection $\mathscr{U} - \{(M, g_{ab})\}$ where (M, g_{ab}) is Minkowski spacetime. Is $(**)$ true or false for $\mathscr{P}$?

We find $(**)$ is true for the collection $\mathscr{P} = \mathscr{U} - \{(M, g_{ab})\}$ where (M, g_{ab}) is Minkowski spacetime. Consider any $(M', g'_{ab}) \in \mathscr{P}$ that is $\mathscr{P}$-extendible. Since (M', g'_{ab}) is $\mathscr{P}$-extendible, it is extendible. Let $(M'', g''_{ab}) \in \mathscr{U}$ be any inextendible extension of (M', g'_{ab}). If $(M'', g''_{ab}) \in \mathscr{P}$, then it must be $\mathscr{P}$-inextendible since it is inextendible. So in this case, (M', g'_{ab}) has a $\mathscr{P}$-inextendible extension. If $(M'', g''_{ab}) \notin \mathscr{P}$, then it is isometric to Minkowski spacetime (M, g_{ab}). So there is a proper isometric embedding $\varphi : M' \to M$ taking the $\mathscr{P}$-extendible (M', g'_{ab}) into (M, g_{ab}). Let $p \in M$ be a point not in $\varphi[M'] \subset M$ and consider $(M - \{p\}, g_{ab})$. This spacetime is not Minkowski spacetime (so it is in $\mathscr{P}$) but has Minkowski spacetime as its only extension (so it is $\mathscr{P}$-inextendible). By construction $(M - \{p\}, g_{ab})$ either extends (M', g'_{ab}) or is isometric to (M', g'_{ab}), but the latter possibility can be ruled out since $(M - \{p\}, g_{ab})$ is $\mathscr{P}$-inextendible and $(M' g'_{ab})$ is not. So in this case too, (M', g'_{ab}) has a $\mathscr{P}$-inextendible extension.

Exercise 36   Let $\mathscr{P} \subset \mathscr{U}$ be the collection of geodesically incomplete spacetimes. For each $\mathscr{P}$-extendible spacetime, find a $\mathscr{P}$-inextendible extension.

Let $\mathscr{P} \subset \mathscr{U}$ be the collection of geodesically incomplete spacetimes and let (M, g_{ab}) be any $\mathscr{P}$-extendible spacetime. Let (M', g'_{ab}) be any $\mathscr{P}$-extension of (M, g_{ab}). If (M', g'_{ab}) is inextendible, then (M', g'_{ab}) is a $\mathscr{P}$-inextendible extension of (M, g_{ab}). If (M', g'_{ab}) is extendible, let (M'', g''_{ab}) be any inextendible extension to it. If (M'', g''_{ab}) is geodesically incomplete, then (M'', g''_{ab}) is a $\mathscr{P}$-inextendible extension of (M, g_{ab}). If (M'', g''_{ab}) is geodesically complete, then consider the spacetime $(M'' - \{p\}, g''_{ab})$ for any point $p \in M'' - M$. We find

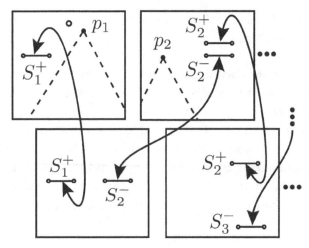

Figure 73 The missing point in the first link of the chain spacetime does not spoil the underdetermination result.

that $(M'' - \{p\}, g''_{ab})$ is geodesically incomplete (since it is extendible) and $\mathscr{P}$-inextendible (since its only extension is the geodesically complete (M'', g''_{ab})). So $(M'' - \{p\}, g''_{ab})$ is a $\mathscr{P}$-inextendible extension of (M, g_{ab}).

Exercise 37 For any $(M, g_{ab}) \in \mathscr{U}$ that is not causally bizarre, find a $(\mathscr{V} - \mathscr{U})$-spacetime (M', g'_{ab}) such that (i) (M, g_{ab}) and (M', g'_{ab}) are locally isometric but not isometric and (ii) (M, g_{ab}) is weakly observationally indistinguishable from (M', g'_{ab}).

Consider any non-causally bizarre spacetime $(M, g_{ab}) \in \mathscr{U}$. Construct a corresponding chain spacetime $(M', g'_{ab}) \in \mathscr{U}$ where (i) (M, g_{ab}) and (M', g'_{ab}) are locally isometric but not isometric and (ii) (M, g_{ab}) is weakly observationally indistinguishable from (M', g'_{ab}) (recall Figure 40). Find a point $q \in M'$ such that $(M' - \{q\}, g'_{ab})$ does not spoil the underdetermination result in the sense that (i) (M, g_{ab}) and $(M' - \{q\}, g'_{ab})$ are locally isometric but not isometric and (ii) (M, g_{ab}) is weakly observationally indistinguishable from $(M' - \{q\}, g'_{ab})$ (see Figure 73). Now consider two copies (M'_1, g'_1) and (M'_2, g'_2) of the original chain spacetime (M', g'_{ab}) and let $\varphi : M'_1 \to M'_2$ be the identity map between the two copies. Let (M'', g''_{ab}) be the result of identifying the point p in (M'_1, g'_1) with the point $\varphi(p)$ in (M'_2, g'_2) for all $p \neq q$. This non-Hausdorff $\mathscr{V}$-spacetime is just (M', g'_{ab}) with a doubled point q. One can verify that (i) (M, g_{ab}) and (M'', g''_{ab}) are locally isometric but not isometric and (ii) (M, g_{ab}) is weakly observationally indistinguishable from (M'', g''_{ab}).

Exercise 38 Find a collection $\mathscr{P} \subset \mathscr{V}$ that renders ($**$) true and contains $\mathscr{W}$ as a proper subcollection.

Let (M, g_{ab}) be the branching Minkowski spacetime that is not in the collection $\mathscr{W}$ due to its bifurcating curves. Let $\mathscr{P} \subset \mathscr{V}$ be the collection $\mathscr{W} \cup \{(M, g_{ab})\}$. Let (M', g'_{ab}) be any $\mathscr{P}$-extendible spacetime. Since (M, g_{ab}) is $\mathscr{P}$-inextendible, we know (M', g'_{ab}) must be in the collection $\mathscr{W}$. So (M', g'_{ab}) must have some $\mathscr{W}$-inextendible extension – call it (M'', g''_{ab}). The spacetime (M'', g''_{ab}) will be $\mathscr{P}$-inextendible unless the branching Minkowski spacetime (M, g_{ab}) extends it. But in that case, (M, g_{ab}) is a $\mathscr{P}$-inextendible extension of (M', g'_{ab}). Either way, (M', g'_{ab}) has a $\mathscr{P}$-inextendible extension that shows ($**$) true for $\mathscr{P}$.

Exercise 39 Find a chronological, flat, inextendible extension of the $t < 0$ portion of Misner spacetime.

For each $n \in \mathbb{Z}$, let (M_n, g_n) be a copy of Misner spacetime in (t, φ) coordinates. From each (M_n, g_n) remove the slit $S_n = \{(t, 0) : t \geq 0\}$. Excluding boundary points, identify the right edge of the slit S_n in (M_n, g_n) with the left edge of the slit S_{n+1} in (M_{n+1}, g_{n+1}) for all $n \in \mathbb{Z}$ (see Figure 74). One can verify that the resulting spacetime is a flat, $\mathscr{U}$-inextendible extension of the $t < 0$ portion of Misner spacetime. It is also chronological (Manchak, 2019).

Exercise 40 Find a two-dimensional $(\mathscr{E}, \mathscr{H})$-machine.

Let (M, g_{ab}) be Misner spacetime in (t, φ) coordinates. Remove the point $p = (0, 0)$ from M and then construct the conformally related inextendible

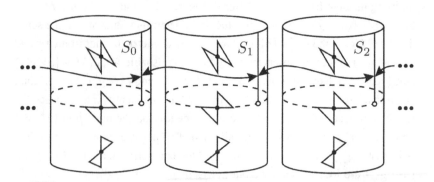

Figure 74 The left edge of the slit S_n is identified with the right edge of the slit S_{n+1} for all $n \in \mathbb{Z}$.

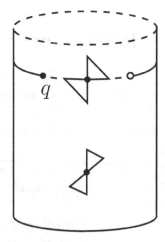

Figure 75 Because of the missing point, the causal past of the point q is not closed.

spacetime $(M - \{p\}, \Omega^2 g_{ab})$ where $\Omega : M - \{p\} \to \mathbb{R}$ is such that it goes to zero as the missing point p is approached along every curve. Now let (M', g'_{ab}) be the $t < 0$ portion of this spacetime that is both globally hyperbolic and $\mathscr{U}$-past-inextendible. Because (M', g'_{ab}) is two-dimensional, it is vacuum and therefore $\mathscr{E}$-past-inextendible. It also has an $\mathscr{E}$-inextendible extension since it has an inextendible extension and we know that all of its extensions are vacuum since they are two-dimensional. Let (M'', g''_{ab}) be any $\mathscr{E}$-inextendible extension to (M', g'_{ab}). Let $q \in M'' - M'$ be a point on the boundary of M' in M''. Because the missing point p must be left out of the extension (M'', g''_{ab}), we find that $\mathscr{J}^-(q)$ cannot be closed (see Figure 75). So the spacetime (M', g'_{ab}) is a $(\mathscr{E}, \mathscr{H})$-machine.

References

Beem, J. (1980). Minkowski space-time is locally extendible. *Communications in Mathematical Physics*, 72(3), 273–275.

Beem, J., Ehrlich, P., & Easley, K. (1996). *Global Lorentzian Geometry*. New York: Marcel Dekker.

Bernal, A. & Sánchez, M. (2007). Globally hyperbolic spacetimes can be defined as "causal" instead of "strongly causal." *Classical and Quantum Gravity*, 24(3), 745–749.

Butterfield, J. (2014). On under-determination in cosmology. *Studies in History and Philosophy of Modern Physics*, 46(1), 57–69.

Carter, B. (1971). Causal structure in spacetime. *General Relativity and Gravitation*, 1(4), 349–391.

Choquet-Bruhat, Y. & Geroch, R. (1969). Global aspects of the Cauchy problem in general relativity. *Communications in Mathematical Physics*, 14(4), 329–335.

Chrusciel, P. & Isenberg, J. (1993). Nonisometric vacuum extensions of vacuum maximal globally hyperbolic spacetimes. *Physical Review D*, 48(4), 1616–1628.

Clarke, C. (1976). Spacetime singularities. *Communications in Mathematical Physics*, 49(1), 17–23.

Clarke, C. (1993). *The Analysis of Space-Time Singularities*. Cambridge: Cambridge University Press.

Clarke, C. & Joshi, P. (1988). On reflecting spacetimes. *Classical and Quantum Gravity*, 5(1), 19–25.

Curiel, E. (1999). The analysis of singular spacetimes. *Philosophy of Science*, 66(Proceedings), S119–S145.

Curiel, E. (2017). A primer on energy conditions. In D. Lehmkuhl, G. Schiemann, & E. Scholz, eds., *Towards a Theory of Spacetime Theories*. Boston: Birkhäuser, 43–104.

Doboszewski, J. (2019). Epistemic holes and determinism in classical general relativity. *British Journal for the Philosophy of Science*. https://doi.org/10.1093/bjps/axz011

Doboszewski, J. (2020). Some other "no hole" spacetimes properties are unstable too. *Foundations of Physics*, 50(5), 379–384.

Earman, J. (1986). *Primer on Determinism*. Dordrecht: Reidel.

Earman, J. (1989). *World Enough and Spacetime: Absolute versus Relational Theories of Space and Time*. Cambridge, MA: MIT Press.

Earman, J. (1995). *Bangs, Crunches, Whimpers, and Shrieks: Singularities and Acausalities in Relativistic Spacetimes*. Oxford: Oxford University Press.

Earman, J. (2001). Lambda: The constant that refuses to die. *Archives for History of Exact Sciences*, 55(3), 189–220.

Earman, J. (2008). Pruning some branches from "branching spacetimes." In D. Dieks, ed., *The Ontology of Spacetime II*. Amsterdam: Elsevier, 187–205.

Earman, J. & Norton, J. (1993). Forever is a day: Supertasks in Pitowsky and Malament-Hogarth spacetimes. *Philosophy of Science*, 60(1), 22–42.

Earman, J., Smeenk, C., & Wüthrich, C. (2009). Do the laws of physics forbid the operation of time machines? *Synthese*, 169(1), 91–124.

Earman, J., Wüthrich, C., & Manchak, J. (2016). Time machines. In E. Zalta, ed., *Stanford Encyclopedia of Philosophy*. https://plato.stanford.edu/ entries/time-machine/

Ellis, G. (1975). Cosmology and verifiability. *Quarterly Journal of the Royal Astronomical Society*, 16(1), 245–264.

Ellis, G. & Schmidt, B. (1977). Singular space-times. *General Relativity and Gravitation*, 8(11), 915–953.

Fletcher, S. (2016). Similarity, topology, and physical significance in relativity theory. *British Journal for the Philosophy of Science*, 67(2), 365–389.

Fletcher S., Manchak, J., Schneider, M., & Weatherall, J. (2018). Would two dimensions be world enough for spacetime? *Studies in History and Philosophy of Modern Physics*, 63(1), 100–113.

Galloway, G. & Ling, E. (2017). Some remarks on the C^0-(in)extendibility of spacetimes. *Annales Henri Poincaré*, 18(1), 3427–3447.

Geroch, R. (1967). Topology in general relativity. *Journal of Mathematical Physics*, 8(4), 782–786.

Geroch, R. (1968a). What is a singularity in general relativity? *Annals of Physics*, 48(3), 526–540.

Geroch, R. (1968b). Structure of singularities. In C. DeWitt & J. Wheeler, eds., *Battelle Rencontres; 1967 Lectures in Mathematics and Physics*. New York: Benjamin Inc., 236–241.

Geroch, R. (1968c). Local characterization of singularities in general relativity. *Journal of Mathematical Physics*, 9(3), 450–465.

Geroch, R. (1969). Limits of spacetimes. *Communications in Mathematical Physics*, 13(3), 180–193.

Geroch, R. (1970a). Singularities. In M. Carmeli, S. Fickler, & L. Witten, eds., *Relativity*. New York: Plenum Press, 259–291.

Geroch, R. (1970b). Domain of dependence. *Journal of Mathematical Physics*, 11(2), 437–449.

Geroch, R. (1971a). Spacetime structure from a global viewpoint. In B. Sachs, ed., *General Relativity and Cosmology*. New York: Academic Press, 71–103.

Geroch, R. (1971b). General relativity in the large. *General Relativity and Gravitation*, 2(1), 61–74.

Geroch, R. (1977). Prediction in general relativity. In J. Earman, C. Glymour, & J. Stachel, eds., *Foundations of Space-Time Theories, Minnesota Studies in the Philosophy of Science, vol. 8*. Minneapolis: University of Minnesota Press, 81–93.

Geroch, R. & Horowitz, G. (1979). Global structure of spacetimes. In S. Hawking & W. Israel, eds., *General Relativity: An Einstein Centenary Survey*. Cambridge: Cambridge University Press, 212–293.

Glymour, C. (1972). Topology, cosmology, and convention. *Synthese*, 24(1), 195–218.

Glymour, C. (1977). Indistinguishable space-times and the fundamental group. In J. Earman, C. Glymour, & J. Stachel, eds., *Foundations of Space-Time Theories, Minnesota Studies in the Philosophy of Science, vol 8*. Minneapolis: University of Minnesota Press, 50–60.

Gödel, K. (1949). An example of a new type of cosmological solutions of Einstein's field equations of gravitation. *Reviews of Modern Physics*, 21(3), 447–450.

Hájíček, P. (1971a). Bifurcate space-times. *Journal of Mathematical Physics*, 12(1), 157–160.

Hájíček, P. (1971b). Causality in non-Hausdorff space-times. *Communications in Mathematical Physics*, 21(1), 75–84.

Hawking, S. (1969). The existence of cosmic time functions. *Proceedings of the Royal Society A*, 308(1494), 433–435.

Hawking, S. (1992). The chronology protection conjecture. *Physical Review D*, 46(2), 603–611.

Hawking, S. & Ellis, G. (1973). *The Large Scale Structure of Space-Time*. Cambridge: Cambridge University Press.

Hawking, S. & Penrose, R. (1970). The singularities of gravitational collapse and cosmology. *Proceedings of the Royal Society A*, 314(1519), 529–548.

Hawking, S. & Sachs, R. (1974). Causally continuous spacetimes. *Communications in Mathematical Physics*, 35(4), 287–296.

Hogarth, M. (1992). Does general relativity allow an observer to view an eternity in a finite time? *Foundations of Physics Letters*, 5(2), 173-181.

Hogarth, M. (1993). Predicting the future in relativistic spacetimes. *Studies in History and Philosophy of Modern Physics*, 24(5), 721–739.

Hogarth, M. (1997). A remark concerning prediction and spacetime singularities. *Studies in History and Philosophy of Modern Physics*, 28(1), 63–71.

Hounnonkpe, R. & Minguzzi, E. (2019). Globally hyperbolic spacetimes can be defined without the "causal" condition. *Classical and Quantum Gravity*, 36(19), 197001.

Krasnikov, S. (2002). No time machines in classical general relativity. *Classical and Quantum Gravity*, 19(15), 4109–4129.

Krasnikov, S. (2009). Even the Minkowski space is holed. *Physical Review D*, 79(12), 124041.

Krasnikov, S. (2018). *Back-in-Time and Faster-than-Light Travel in General Relativity*. Cham: Springer Nature.

Kronheimer, E. & Penrose, R. (1967). On the structure of causal spaces. *Proceedings of the Cambridge Philosophical Society*, 63(2), 481–501.

Low, R. (2012). Time machines, maximal extensions and Zorn's lemma. *Classical and Quantum Gravity*, 29(9), 097001.

Malament, D. (1977a). Observationally indistinguishable space-times. In J. Earman, C. Glymour, & J. Stachel, eds., *Foundations of Space-Time Theories. Minnesota Studies in the Philosophy of Science, vol. 8*. Minneapolis: University of Minnesota Press, 61–80.

Malament, D. (1977b). The class of continuous timelike curves determines the topology of spacetime. *Journal of Mathematical Physics*, 18(7), 1399–1404.

Malament, D. (2012). *Topics in the Foundations of General Relativity and Newtonian Gravitation Theory*. Chicago: University of Chicago Press.

Manchak, J. (2008). Is prediction possible in general relativity? *Foundations of Physics*, 38(4), 317–321.

Manchak, J. (2009). Can we know the global structure of spacetime? *Studies in History and Philosophy of Modern Physics*, 40(1), 53–56.

Manchak, J. (2011a). What is a physically reasonable spacetime? *Philosophy of Science*, 78(3), 410–420.

Manchak, J. (2011b). No no go: A remark on time machines. *Studies in History and Philosophy of Modern Physics*, 42(1), 74–76.

Manchak, J. (2014a). On space-time singularities, holes, and extensions. *Philosophy of Science*, 81(5), 1066–1076.

Manchak, J. (2014b). Time (hole?) machines. *Studies in History and Philosophy of Modern Physics*, 48(B), 124–127.

Manchak, J. (2016a). Epistemic "holes" in space-time. *Philosophy of Science*, 83(2), 265–276.

Manchak, J. (2016b). On Gödel and the ideality of time. *Philosophy of Science*, 83(5), 1050–1058.

Manchak, J. (2016c). Is the universe as large as it can be? *Erkenntnis*, 81(6), 1341–1344.

Manchak, J. (2018a). Some "no hole" spacetime properties are unstable. *Foundations of Physics*, 48(11), 1539–1545.

Manchak, J. (2018b). Malament-Hogarth machines. *British Journal for the Philosophy of Science*. https://doi.org/10.1093/bjps/axy023.

Manchak, J. (2019). A remark on "time machines" in honor of Howard Stein. *Studies in History and Philosophy of Modern Physics*, 48(1), 111–116.

Manchak, J. (forthcoming). General relativity as a collection of collections of models. Forthcoming in J. Madarász & G. Székely eds., *Hajnal Andréka and Istvań Németi on Unity of Science: From Computing to Relativity Theory through Algebraic Logic*.

Manchak, J. & Roberts, B. (2016). Supertasks. In E. Zalta, ed., *Stanford Encyclopedia of Philosophy*. https://plato.stanford.edu/entries/spacetime-supertasks/.

Minguzzi, E. (2012). Causally simple inextendible spacetimes are hole-free. *Journal of Mathematical Physics*, 53(6), 062501.

Minguzzi, E. (2019). Lorentzian causality theory. *Living Reviews in Relativity*, 22(1), article 3.

Minguzzi, E. & Sánchez, M. (2008). The causal hierarchy of space-times. In D. Alekseevsky & H. Baum, eds., *Recent Developments in Pseudo-Riemannian Geometry*. Zurich: European Mathematical Society, 299–358.

Misner, C. (1967). Taub-NUT spacetime as a counterexample to almost anything. In J. Ehlers, ed., *Relativity Theory and Astrophysics: I. Relativity and Cosmology, Lectures in Applied Mathematics, vol. 8*. Providence, RI: American Mathematical Society, 160–169.

Norton J. (2011). Observationally indistinguishable spacetimes: A challenge for any inductivist. In G. Morgan, ed., *Philosophy of Science Matters: The Philosophy of Peter Achinstein*. Oxford: Oxford University Press, 164–176.

O'Neill, B. (1983). *Semi-Riemannian Geometry with Applications to Relativity*. London: Academic Press.

Penrose, R. (1965). Gravitational collapse and space-time singularities. *Physical Review Letters*, 14(3), 57.

Penrose, R. (1968). Structure of spacetime. In C. DeWitt & J. Wheeler, eds., *Battelle Rencontres; 1967 Lectures in Mathematics and Physics*. New York: Benjamin Inc., 121–235.

Penrose, R. (1969). Gravitational collapse: The role of general relativity. *Revisita del Nuovo Cimento* 1(1): 252–276.

Penrose, R. (1972). *Techniques of Differential Topology in Relativity*. Philadelphia: Society for Industrial and Applied Mathematics.

Penrose, R. (1979). Singularities and time-asymmetry. In S. Hawking & W. Israel, eds., *General Relativity: An Einstein Centenary Survey*. Cambridge: Cambridge University Press, 581–638.

Penrose, R. (1999). The question of cosmic censorship. *Journal of Astrophysics and Astronomy*, 20(3–4), 233–248.

Sbierski, J. (2018). On the proof of the C^0-inextendibility of the Schwarzschild spacetime. *Journal of Physics: Conference Series*, 968(1), 012012.

Steen, L. & Seebach, J. (1970). *Counterexamples in Topology*. New York: Springer.

Wald, R. (1984). *General Relativity*. Chicago: University of Chicago Press.

Acknowledgments

I would like to thank a number of people. First, I thank my global structure teachers for their direction and encouragement: John Earman, Bob Geroch, and David Malament. They have helped me enormously. I thank the series editor, Jim Weatherall, for all of his generous support and the editorial staff at Cambridge for their work with the manuscript. I thank two anonymous referees who provided useful comments on an earlier draft. I thank many colleagues for their assistance at various stages: Hajnal Andréka, Jeff Barrett, Thomas Barrett, Gordon Belot, Jeremy Butterfield, Craig Callender, Chris Clarke, Erik Curiel, Juliusz Doboszewski, George Ellis, Arthur Fine, Sam Fletcher, Clark Glymour, Hans Halvorson, Mark Hogarth, Serguei Krasnikov, Martin Lesourd, Judit Madarász, Ettore Minguzzi, István Németi, John Norton, Josh Norton, Miklós Rédei, Bryan Roberts, Laura Ruetsche, Steve Savitt, Jan Sbierski, Chris Smeenk, Gergely Székely, Giovanni Valente, Bob Wald, and Chris Wüthrich. I thank former students for providing excellent feedback in seminar: Clara Bradley, Elliott Chen, Adam Chin, Ben Feintzeig, Zach Flouris, David Freeborn, Marian Gilton, Kevin Kadowaki, Helen Meskhidze, David Mwakima, Toni Queck, Sarita Rosenstock, Tim Schmitz, Mike Schneider, and Jingyi Wu. Finally, I thank my friends and family – especially June and Meka – for their light and love along the way. This book is dedicated to Meka.

Cambridge Elements ⹀

The Philosophy of Physics

James Owen Weatherall
University of California, Irvine

James Owen Weatherall is Professor of Logic and Philosophy of Science at the University of California, Irvine. He is the author, with Cailin O'Connor, of *The Misinformation Age: How False Beliefs Spread* (Yale, 2019), which was selected as a *New York Times* Editors' Choice and Recommended Reading by *Scientific American*. His previous books were *Void: The Strange Physics of Nothing* (Yale, 2016) and the *New York Times* bestseller *The Physics of Wall Street: A Brief History of Predicting the Unpredictable* (Houghton Mifflin Harcourt, 2013). He has published approximately fifty peer-reviewed research articles in journals in leading physics and philosophy of science journals and has delivered more than 100 invited academic talks and public lectures.

About the Series

This Cambridge Elements series provides concise and structured introductions to all the central topics in the philosophy of physics. The Elements in the series are written by distinguished senior scholars and bright junior scholars with relevant expertise, producing balanced, comprehensive coverage of multiple perspectives in the philosophy of physics.

Cambridge Elements $^{\equiv}$

The Philosophy of Physics

Elements in the Series

Global Spacetime Structure
JB Manchak